MARY DUNN

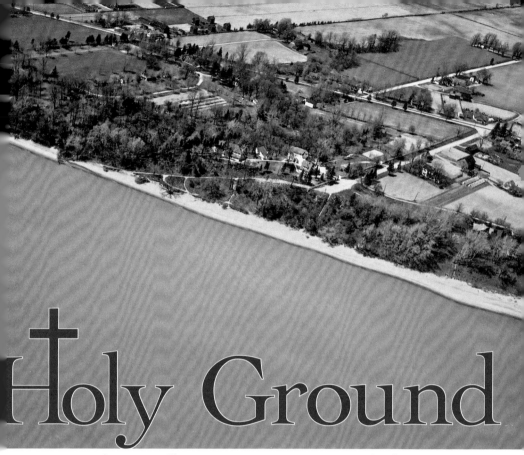

Holy Ground

Holy Family Retreat House and the
Retreat Movement in the Diocese of London

Michael R. Prieur

Further copies of this book can be obtained for $14.95 plus $4.25 tax, handling, and postage by writing to the author:

     Michael Prieur
     St. Peter's Seminary
     1040 Waterloo Street
     London ON N6A 3Y1
     Canada
     tel. 519 432-1824 ext. 223
     mprieur@uwo.ca

Library and Archives Canada Cataloguing in Publication

Prieur, Michael R., 1940-
    Holy ground : Holy Family Retreat House and the retreat movement in the Diocese of London / Michael Prieur.

Includes bibliographical references and index.
ISBN 978-0-9737533-1-8

    1. Holy Family Retreat House (Oxley, Ont.)--History.
2. Spiritual retreat centers--Ontario--Oxley--History.
3. Spiritual retreats--Catholic Church. I. Title.

BX2375.A4P75 2011   269'.60971331   C2011-903687-8

Design: Brian Grebow, BG Communications (www.WeAreYourType.com)
Index: Brian Grebow

Printed in Canada

TABLE *of* CONTENTS

ACKNOWLEDGEMENTS

I AM INDEBTED to many people who helped me to write this book. I begin with all the previous retreat house directors whom I have featured in the book. Their deep faith and evangelical spirit has moved me greatly over the years and inspired the book. Also, the seminary spiritual directors who have come to Oxley over the years have moved my heart to grow in appreciating the many wonderful dimensions here, especially the lay staff, the support workers and the religious men and women who have served here.

My generous readers have included Bishop Ronald Fabbro, Bishop John Michael Sherlock, Fr. Larry Paré, Dr. David Howie, Fr. Michael O'Brien, Fr. Murray Watson, Michael Tremblay, Helen Hodson, and Ruth Beitia. I am also indebted to Jack and Louise Boyde for reading the text and for Louise's wonderful proofreading skills. David Johnston, a seminarian from Port Lambton, generously typed out many pages of the "Affirmations" stories featured in the book. Brian Grebow has done another remarkable job designing and producing the book. (He also created my book, *Panes of Glory.*) His wife, Dr. Roberta (Robbi) Howlett, generously acted as an exceptional substantive editor for the book. Jo-Ann Slawik, our indefatigable receptionist at the seminary, has handled countless electronic needs for me. Debra Majer, our diocesan archivist, provided invaluable materials from the diocesan archives. To all these grand people, I am truly grateful.

Finally, I am deeply indebted to Fr. Ted Gatfield, who has co-sponsored the project with me. His delightful wit and wisdom, along with his deep faith, have been a deep source of grace to me in the writing of the book. Our mutual visit to see Fr. Meloche in California just before he died, provided an invaluable link for both of us to the "original grace" of the retreat house directors. The result of all of this is that we have become real friends, and I treasure this most of all.

I take full responsibility for the way I have used the information in this book. In my efforts to put a lighter touch into the text, I pray that I have not offended anyone. If so, I ask their forgiveness. If I have made any factual errors, I ask you to let me know, and they will be corrected in any subsequent editions. The text was not intended to be definitive. I believe in leaving more joy for someone else in researching and correcting this delightful story.

My big wish is that our collective efforts will galvanize all of us to do all we can to support spiritual retreats in our diocese. Coming away to rest a while with the Lord is indispensable if we wish to stay close to the Lord. To one and all of my faithful supporters, may God fill you with "Holy Ground" in your hearts.

I also wish to thank Fr. Michael O'Brien, the present "priest-in-residence" at the retreat house, for doing many significant small tasks in assisting me to do the book. Not to be forgotten are my invaluable proofreaders and women of prayer, the Sisters of the Precious Blood, here in London, Ontario. They have hopefully kept any mistakes to the minimum of three, which they maintain will happen in any book! God bless them all!

CREDIT IS DUE to the following for generously providing the pictures for this book: Debra Majer for pictures from the diocesan archives; Fr. Gary Ducharme for many of the nature photos and shots of the buildings and grounds; the successors of "Giffels Associates" for verbal permission to print the blueprint of the "Dream Retreat House;" Gerry Pouget for permission to use materials on Oxley from their wonderful book, *Harrow and Colchester South 1792–1992* (Harrow History Book Committee, 1993); *The Windsor Star* for permission to print the photos of Fr. Gatfield on page 58 and of Fr. Jansen on pp. 78 and 84; Sr. Shirley McAuley, Sr. Rosie Rau and the Ursuline Sisters for their pictures in Chapter 8; the Sisters of St. Joseph and Ruth Beitia of the Institute of Secular Missionaries for the pictures they provided of the women in their Institute and with Fr. Jansen; Fr. Charlie Beuglet and Jeanne Ryan, sister of Fr. Beuglet, for photos dealing with life at the retreat house in the late 60s; Victor Aziz and Barry Callow for the photo of the Nazareth painting of Philip Aziz; John Coderre for pictures of Fr. Dan Rocheleau and his friends; Al Janisse for pictures of retreatants at Oxley; the diocesan and seminary archives for some historical data and pictures of the early years of the retreat house; Fr. Michael O'Brien for pictures of the retreatants in 2010 and for the picture of the present retreat house staff; and especially Fr. Ted Gatfield for the pictures from the banquet scenes and speakers at the Prince Edward Hotel in the 1960s in Chapter 5, and for the aerial shot of the retreat house on the title page inside the cover.

If I have not adequately acknowledged anyone else's work, please let me know and I will redress this in future editions of the book.

introduction

You know you need a break. You feel overwhelmed, tired, torn apart by the frenetic pace of the twenty-first century. So many hats to wear at work … so many rapid changes … so much uncertainty … so many crumbling companies and institutional changes … so many failed marriages and broken promises. Someone says to you: "You need a retreat!" A timeless lightning bolt from God.

Driving from a distance, Holy Family Retreat House seems almost impossible to find. But at last, the final turn off County Road 50 in the hamlet of Oxley leads to parking spaces right next to a bluff. Below, waves splash from Lake Erie. On a clear night, the lights of Sandusky, Ohio, are visible in the sky. Dragging your suitcase behind you, an inscription on a vine-draped, stone arch over the sidewalk beckons to your weary soul.

The arch at the entrance way

"You are standing on Holy Ground" is emblazoned at the top. Your soul aches for something apart (the meaning of "holy"), peaceful, soothing, to assuage the unsettling chaos inside you. You breathe a weak prayer: "Lord, my heart is heavy. Help me."

You trudge up the sidewalk beside a house on the left with clean white siding. A few meters ahead, a "Welcome" sign directs you to an entrance into a larger white building on the right. You open the well-fit door, and the gentle smile of one of the retreat house staff tells you instantly that God's restful love lives here. Already, your heavy burden seems lighter.

* * *

Holy Family Retreat House has been the focus of spiritual renewal for thousands of people since opening in 1948. It has maintained its presence in spite

All are welcome here.

of its precarious location on a seemingly tiny spit of land between Lake Erie and the deep ravine behind it. Resourceful directors and supporters have been amazing in their efforts to scrounge just about everything in order to survive. Countless individuals, convinced of the need for a retreat location in the southwest portion of the Diocese of London, rallied to the cause. For over sixty years, this labour of love has been God's instrument for physical and spiritual rejuvenation. It is time to tell the story of this amazing oasis of grace.

St. Peter's Seminary has offered an eight-day directed retreat at Holy Family Retreat House for its students and others since 1974. In April of that first year, Fr. Jack O'Flaherty and I cajoled the deacon class at the seminary to experience an Ignatian retreat after both of us had made the thirty-day retreat and ten-day institute at Guelph the previous year. With the help of Fr. Peter LeBlanc, S.J., we led that first retreat. Fr. Adrian Jansen was the director then of the retreat house. As this kind of retreat continued year after year, he would join our retreat team for one evening to tell stories, share the contents of a good bottle of scotch, and fill us in on various aspects of the retreat house history. As they say, "It all comes out with the cork!"

After hearing these stories for over thirty years, it finally dawned on me: someone has to write this down for posterity. This "oasis of grace" deserves a public forum. The book was conceived in my creative heart.

By the providence of God, Fr. Ted Gatfield and I were able to spend a week in August 2007 with the founding director, Fr. Art Meloche, in his nursing home in San Diego, California. His elephantine memory filled in many lacunae from my recent interviews with the other directors and staff members. At ninety-two years of age, he may not always have been right but he *was* certain! He was a joy to behold. He died in May of the following year.

Holy Family Retreat House is holy ground. But even more holy are the people who have made it possible. And this holiness has been passed on to all those who have spent any time praying and pondering here. Today, what our world needs most is to pause and reflect *in silence.* Our people, especially our young ones, are immersed in constant noise. We all need to realize that God's word most often comes to our souls in silence, that interior silence which allows his still, small voice to be heard and acted upon.

It is my fervent wish that this book, first and foremost, will be a visible sign of gratitude to the entire retreat house "family." Their stories must be told to recognize their huge sacrifices, made to enable the retreat house to both survive and thrive. I do not intend this work to be a scholarly, definitive thesis. I would rather like it to be a popular presentation of a great deal of oral and some written traditions which need to be assembled and put to print while some of these "giants" are still with us. I leave the academic thesis to a budding new church historian looking for a topic.

Writing history, when most of the personae are still living, is dangerous stuff! The point is, for most of these stories, *I was not there!* So, I must apologize in advance for any errors or omissions in this work. I have tried to speak with as many individuals as reasonably possible to get the work done after this idea has germinated in me for so long. I have tried to include as many names and pictures as possible for a work of this length. I have endeavoured to present the facts without damaging anyone's good name. If anything is amiss, please let me know and I will gladly make an *errata* insertion for this edition and make the necessary changes if another edition is born.

My second aim is to clarify the influence of the Holy Spirit in the whole "lay retreat movement"—both internationally and in our diocese—for almost a century. The origins of this movement are relatively unknown to our people today, origins that provide insights for our own call to holiness in our diocese.[1] Making some fresh historical connections has given me new enthusiasm in seeing how the Spirit has been, and is, at work weaving various threads together in the tapestry of our own diocesan spiritual growth. These connections can be prescient for our diocesan spiritual renewal, as well as for

---

1   Goal # 1 of the Diocesan Pastoral Plan: "As living signs of Christ's presence, we will respond to the call to personal holiness given to all by committing ourselves to opportunities for ongoing conversion and spiritual renewal." See the website for the Diocese of London <http://wp.dol.ca/webportal/diocese/home/1>.

envisioning the future for our own retreat house, something that is happening as I write these pages.

Finally, I hope the book will be an incentive for others to bring their heavy hearts and deepest yearnings to this holy ground, or indeed any other holy ground, for a quiet retreat in order to be refreshed, inspired and encouraged by God. Blaise Pascal once said something like, "All of the world's problems could be resolved if man could learn to be alone in his room." Erich Fromm had a similar insight in his classic work *The Art of Loving*—"The ability to be alone is the condition for the ability to love." Of course, the Psalmist nails it down succinctly: "Be still and know that I am God." (*Ps.* 46:10) Silent retreats are the healing balm for our souls.

The sign next to a weathered wooden yoke suspended outside the door of Nazareth House, donated by Fr. Martin "Sam" Johnson, beckons us all:

"Come to me all you who are burdened.

I will refresh you." (*Matt.* 11:28)

May Holy Family Retreat House, and this book, continue to refresh your hearts through God, Father, Son and Holy Spirit, as well as Mary and Joseph for whom Jesus had such tender love.

Michael Prieur
March 25, 2011
Feast of the Annunciation

Affirmations

At Oxley I am like a pilgrim – no maps, no itinerary, simply hold onto the hand of God, The Great Pilgrim, and travel with hope that one day I can understand the benefits and pass them on to others.

It's not about Holy Family Retreat Centre, it's about what happens being here – what takes place in my heart.

God Bless all the special people working here, they make it happen and always with such kindness, understanding and cheer.

THANK YOU!

M.D.

June 10, 2008

Coming here is like coming out of a storm – or recovering from a draining sickness.

This morning, it was raining. But even with that, I felt a delightful freshness. I am grateful for the peace, the healing and new hope that is offered here. Thanks to Fr. Des, Fr. Gary and staff.

Gratefully Fr. L.H.

March 12, 2006

This place is truly hallowed ground. A place to just let go! to cry, to wash away the old, bad, ugliness, to wash away to be clean, to begin again. Each day a new beginning, a new start, today is the first day of the rest of my life, to live it the way I want to, the way God had extended it for me. Thank you Lord for this opportunity, thank for all the earthly hands + hearts that made this possible. Thank you for womanhood that has its own special and unique qualities. Thank you for loving ME!

B.

Jul 17-19, 09
Grief Recovery Retreat

I love the deep silence of the Oasis. There's a great Something in this Nothing.

C.L.

chapter 1

The Retreat Movement in the 1930s and 1940s

In the first part of the twentieth century, Catholics realized more and more that they needed to make spiritual retreats every year to deepen their faith. St. Ignatius Loyola (1491–1556), the founder of the Jesuits, wrote a spiritual classic called *The Spiritual Exercises.*[1] Intended primarily for people in religious life, these days of prayer usually lasted for thirty days. However, shorter versions became necessary for lay people, resulting in retreats lasting anywhere from a weekend to a week or more. Lay people were also discovering the value of regular personal retreats for their spiritual lives. The Holy Spirit was moving.

Pope Pius XI (1922–1939)

In 1929, Pope Pius XI wrote an encyclical extolling the necessity of taking extended periods of time to make the exercises.[2] He specifically mentions "Retreats for Workmen" as well as "Associated Sodalities of Perseverance."[3] He also invited the laity in general to do the same, according to their individual circumstances of time and availability. What he said then could just as easily be said today (but in shorter sentences!):

---

1 See Louis J. Puhl, S.J., *The Spiritual Exercises of St. Ignatius*, Chicago, Illinois, Loyola University Press, 1951.

2 Pius XI, Encyclical Letter *Mens nostra*, Dec. 20, 1929, in Claudia Carlen, IHM, ed., *The Papal Encyclicals, 1903–1939*, Raleigh, Va., McGrath Publishing Co., 1981, pp. 335–343.

3 *Ibid.*, n. 12.

"Let all those remain as a manifest proof, how, whether drawn by the beauty of a more holy and more perfect life, or tossed by the turbid tempests of the time, or moved by the solicitudes of life, or beset by the frauds and fallacies of the world, or fighting against the deadly plague of Rationalism, or allured by the fascination of the senses, withdrawing themselves into those holy houses, have tasted again the peace of solitude, all the sweeter to them because of the heavy labours they have borne, and meditating on heavenly things, have ordered their life in accordance with supernatural lessons."[4]

This pope, who wrote the famous encyclical on social justice, *Quadragesimo Anno* (May 15, 1931), was convinced that people involved in any kind of Catholic Action needed to make some kind of retreat to ensure that their activity in Catholic Action was grounded in prayer and dependence on God. His timeless and valid intuition was a corroboration of the burgeoning lay retreat movement, especially in North America.

On December 29, 1934, the apostolic delegate to the United States, the Most Rev. Amleto Giovanni Cicognani, gave a talk to the National Conference of the Laymen's Retreat Movement in Washington, D.C. He proclaimed that the retreat movement is "one of the choicest activities of Catholic action." His talk cribbed large sections of the encyclical of Pius XI, *Mens nostra*, for his audience. The talk was summarized in *The Catholic Record,* the official newspaper of the London diocese.[5] It is clear that we have two strong currents converging: a need felt by lay people to make retreats, and an encouraging hierarchy to promote and officially authenticate this need. It is an excellent example of a down to earth *consensus fidelium,* that deep, unified conviction in *both* clergy and laity of what the Spirit is urging us to believe and practice in our Christian lives.

The Lay Retreat Movement in the Diocese of London

Fr. Art Meloche gives us a wonderful historical note on what happened in our own diocese. "The history of the Lay Retreat Movement in the Diocese of London began officially in the summer of 1935. At that time Fr. Augustine Cotter of the Congregation of the Passion was invited to preach a retreat to a group of 21 laymen at St. Peter's Seminary. His Excellency, the Most Rev. Philip F. Pocock, D.D., Bishop of Saskatoon, then a priest of St. Peter's Seminary, became interested in the group. A short time after this retreat, Fr. Pocock was appointed diocesan director of closed retreats for laymen."

---

4   *Ibid.,* n. 7.

5   "The Retreat Movement: Apostolic Delegate Terms It Choice Activity of Catholic Action", *The Catholic Record,* Jan. 19, 1935, p. 3.

He continues: "Laymen of the London Diocese, however, had been making retreats for some years previous to 1935. In the year 1914, Leo Page of Windsor joined a group of four Windsor men who went to St. Stanislaus' Retreat House in Cleveland to make his first retreat under the direction of Fr. Theodore VanRossum, S.J. Under his leadership and assisted by Harry Gignac, K.S.G. of Windsor, a group of businessmen began making an annual retreat at Cleveland."[6] It is interesting to see the ongoing connection with the seminary in this whole saga. Along with this is the introduction of a remarkable Catholic layman, Leo Page. He is worth more than a passing reference.

A men's retreat group on the front steps of St. Peter's Seminary

Fr. Cotter (left) and Fr. Philip Pocock (right) with original group of retreatants at the seminary

Leo Page (1871–1951): "Father of Retreats" in the London Diocese

When you come into the door of the breezeway in St. Joseph's Building, a beautifully carved wooden plaque catches your attention. Crafted by the late Dr. Honoré Schiller, this warm image of Leo Page attracts your curiosity. A

6   Rev. A.L. Meloche, "Record of Retreats in London Diocese," unidentified newspaper article in Diocesan Archives.

LEO PAGE
1871 - 1951
Father of Retreats

notebook on a shelf under it, prepared by Rosemary Schiller, Dr. Schiller's wife and related to Leo Page, opens up the story. The "Father of Retreats," who "founded the Laymen's Retreat League in the Diocese of London,"[7] steps forward from the pages.

He was born in 1871 in Saginaw, Michigan. His family moved to the Border Cities when he was eighteen months old. His early schooling included public school in Sandwich, Ontario, secondary school in old Windsor High School on the corner of Goyeau and Park Streets, known as the "Soup Kitchen."

He delivered newspapers, giving him the idea of founding the Goodfellows Club. Beginning in 1914, they sold a newspaper at Christmas time every year, the proceeds going to needy individuals. He had an enterprising spirit. This also led him to open several general stores, one in Sandwich in 1891, and another in Ojibway in 1898.

In 1911, his warm and engaging personality enabled him to form a syndicate with T.A. Morton, his brother the late R.M. Morton, A.F. Healy, A. Chappus, and himself. In 1913, they bought 85 acres of land where Hall and Moy Avenues are now, gradually sold off the property for houses, and made a good profit. His business acumen snowballed. In 1928, he became president of Purity Dairies (Home of "Pure as a Lily" Milk), and shortly after of the Butternut Bread Company (later sold to Canada Bread). The Page family home was on Ouellette Avenue, where Janisse Brothers Funeral Home now is. It was described as "quite the prettiest place in all the Border Cities. It is done in California Style." Leo Page could be called a Windsor tycoon, but with a big difference.

He exuded energy and joy, with a merry twinkle in his eye. He was a man

---

7   The small plaque at the base of the 14th Station of the Cross on the grounds has inscribed on it: Gift/Leo Page/"Father of Retreats." The material in this section on Leo Page is drawn from the materials in this binder. Most of the articles are without source references, making it difficult to cite the references quoted herein.

with an understanding heart. He was always looking for an opportunity to bring a little sunshine into people's lives. At the Kiwanis Camp in Port Dover, where he had a summer cottage, the folks there gave him the sobriquet "The Sucker Man." For over thirteen years he was always handing out lollipop suckers to the kiddies. Later in life, when vacationing in Arizona, he was called "Santa Claus." Every day on his vacation, he would take four young men for a ride in his automobile. They were in the local sanatorium, being treated for tuberculosis. His generosity abounded. In 1929, his syndicate donated 55 acres of land to allow St. Mary's Academy to be built.

However, it was his deeply rooted spiritual life that made him a tycoon with a difference. As we said earlier, the retreat movement in the Diocese of London began with a small group of Windsor men over thirty years before the retreat house opened in Oxley in 1948.[8] From 1914 to 1936, each summer Leo Page used to take a group of professional men, often on his yacht, from Windsor to Cleveland. Besides Sir Harry E. Gignac, K.S.G., they also included George and Armand Janisse and Dr. Paul Poisson. They grew from a half-dozen or so to more than seventy men who made this annual trip by boat or car. This continued until the outbreak of World War II, when the Cleveland retreats had to be abandoned due to the wartime foreign exchange regulations.

Leo Page managed the "Windsor Laymen's Retreats" during this time. People mentioned that he never coaxed anyone to make a retreat with him. Those who went on retreat truly wanted to go. They wanted the spiritual benefit that would be derived from such a retreat. He used to say, "If you are too busy to pray, you are too busy." Upon his retirement from this role in 1936, he received a wonderful accolade from one of the Ohio Jesuits, Fr. W.A. Mitchell, for his careful planning and devoted attention to the retreats in Cleveland. He gave a "Last Word" to him: "Do not let the work lag; pray for it, labor for it, think of it, encourage it and God will do the rest. I shall not forget you, and I shall say three Masses for you in the near future."[9]

After he resigned, a committee was set up to continue making arrangements for these retreats. These men included H.E. Gignac, James E. Wall, Thomas Cada, Kenneth Brooks, Oswald Murphy and W. J. Haslam. The jovial "Founding Father" had generated a powerful spiritual retreat family. The stage was set for the retreat movement to keep moving forward in the diocese.

---

8   See "Lay Retreats in London Diocese," *The Catholic Record*, July 17, 1937, p. 5. For this section, the author acknowledges the assistance of Peter Meehan and his concurrent research in *The Catholic Record* while working on his book on Archbishop Pocock in the summer of 2007 at the seminary.

9   Letter in the diocesan archives.

Sir Harry Gignac was a Knight of St. Gregory.

Growing Retreats in the London Diocese

In the meantime, following the example of the Windsor group, laymen in other parts of the diocese were interested in making retreats. "During one year, the former Bishop of London, His Excellency the Most Rev. Michael F. Fallon, D.D., personally conducted the exercises of a retreat for the group at Assumption College, Windsor. During another year when this group was unable to go to Cleveland, their annual retreat was conducted in Toronto, at the House of the Jesuits. However, this group, at the invitation of the diocesan director, Fr. Pocock, began in 1939 to make their annual retreat at St. Peter's Seminary, London. This group still forms the leadership of the English-speaking men of Windsor district."[10]

Also in 1939, a retreat was attempted at St. Alphonsus Seminary, Woodstock. However, this venture was discontinued when the men made known their intention to make their retreats at St. Peter's Seminary in London.

The retreat movement also blossomed among French-speaking laymen as well. On August 8, 1927 a group of 21 men gathered at Manresa, the Jesuit Retreat House just outside of Detroit, Michigan. Fr. Louis Lalande, S.J., former rector of the Collège Sainte Marie at Montréal, Québec, conducted the exercises. Dennis Janisse, of Windsor, Ontario, was named president of the organization. Other officers were Gustace LaCasse, M.D., vice-president; Leon Lalande, secretary; and Ulysse G. Reaume, treasurer, with Ferdinand C. Parent and J.L. Bacicot as directors. In 1928 there were 23 who made the retreat. In 1929 there were two retreats with 18 members each. In 1931 this group began to make the retreat at Assumption College, Windsor. In 1939, at the invitation of Fr. Pocock, these laymen began to make the retreat at St. Peter's Seminary, London. These French retreats saw their largest number at the seminary in 1948 with a whopping number of 123 men.

10 Rev. A. L. Meloche, "Record of Retreats in London Diocese," unidentified newspaper article in London diocese archives. The following section is also from this article.

Fr. Philip Pocock

We have been mentioning this seminary director of retreats frequently in this section. It is time to do a mini-portrait of this remarkable priest in this period of his life.

A men's and women's retreat at St. Peter's Seminary

As we mentioned earlier, in 1935 Bishop John Thomas Kidd assigned Fr. Philip Pocock, professor of Moral Theology at that time at St. Peter's Seminary, to take charge of diocesan retreats. As a result of this appointment, he was able to oversee some of these retreats, which were held in the summertime at the new St. Peter's Seminary, opened in north London in 1926.

Bishop Kidd made a wise choice in Fr. Pocock. Fr. Art Meloche, his pro-tégé, had fond memories of him. He was very quiet, kind, and never shouted at any time. He was always quite serious, yet a real communicator. In the seminary, everyone would go to him for some kind of spiritual direction. In his classes, he made moral theology tremendously interesting, even throwing in challenging "trick questions" in his oral exams. He had a keen intellect and was the number one teacher at the seminary. He was a good administrator and worked very well with lay people. He was a good organizer and even an excellent handball player. Basically, he was a happy man. When he met you, he made you feel important to him. It is not surprising that he was able to combine moral theology with the spirituality needed to allow the fledgling retreat movement to grow in the London diocese.

More and More Retreats

In June of 1937, Mrs. U. Durocher organized a group of women from the Windsor district to make the first women's summer retreat at

Bishop Philip Pocock in 1944

Brescia Hall (now called Brescia University College) in London. Another one was organized in September. Also, Fr. W. Langlois, pastor of Ste. Rose of Lima parish in the former Riverside, Ontario, and Fr. E. Chavalier, pastor of Our Lady of the Lake parish (later known as Our Lady of the Rosary parish) in old Walkerville, Ontario, led a large group of Essex County men for the first annual French retreat held at the seminary. Formerly, a number of Windsor parishioners made monthly retreats at Assumption College, and this nucleus was also expected to attract others to make these retreats. More and more men and women continued to take advantage of these annual retreats.

In 1938, Bishop Kidd extended the Lay Retreat Movement in the diocese. He made the following appointments: Fr. W.J. Langlois, assisted by Fr. E. Chevalier, organizer of retreats in the French language; Fr. P.A. Mugan, organizer of English retreats for the men of Windsor and district; Fr. W.T. O'Rourke, organizer of the annual Labour Day Retreat for the men of the diocese; Fr. J.A. Feeney, organizer of retreats for the women of London; and Fr. J. Austin Roney, organizer of retreats for the women of Windsor and district, business girls and diocesan women. He also indicated that within a short time, everyone would receive information regarding summer retreats from Fr. Philip Pocock, Diocesan Director. It was the Bishop's wish that a considerable number of parishioners would make a "closed retreat," meaning a retreat with complete silence.[11]

The numbers are significant: two retreats were held at St. Mary's Academy, Windsor, and two retreats at Brescia Hall, London. In 1946, Fr. Meloche tells us there were 62 married women and 172 business girls who made retreats at the Academy. Brescia Hall boasted of 55 married women and 183 business women making four retreats there. Rev. F. Mulkern of Windsor was the priest director for the women's retreats and Rev. C. Petit of St. Peter's Cathedral, London, for women in the London district. Sr. M. Electa of the Congregation of the Holy Names of Jesus and Mary, Windsor, directed the Windsor groups and Mother Gertrude of the Ursuline community directed the London group.

Some of these retreats were organized in the parishes. French retreats were held in St. Joachim and Paincourt. The format of the parish retreats retained the element of silence from the weekend retreats, but these were only for one day, since the parishes lacked facilities for any overnight stay for the retreatants. They would gather on a Sunday morning, listen to talks, celebrate Mass with a special retreat sermon and then finish with a talk in the evening, concluding with Benediction. Today, we might call this a "Day of Prayer."

Some people could not get away from their work at the dates set for the weekends of the London retreats. These individuals would go to the Manresa

11 "Appointments for London Lay Retreats," *The Catholic Record*, May 7, 1938, p. 1.

House of Retreats in Birmingham, Michigan. This also included a group of French-speaking retreatants.

Bishop Kidd further encouraged retreats for Catholic lay teachers of the diocese of London in 1938. The Ursuline Religious of the diocese of London offered Brescia Hall for retreats for teachers of the diocese. The Holy Name Sisters of Windsor did likewise with St. Mary's Academy. Both retreats began on the evening of Wednesday, June 29 and concluded on Saturday, July 2. Some two hundred teachers of the diocese were divided into two groups, the Windsor group using the Academy and the London/Chatham/Stratford group Brescia Hall in London.

The Catholic Layman's Retreat Movement

People were clearly hungering for retreats in North America in the 30s. Blossoming side by side with the Catholic Action Movement, both clergy and laity realized that Catholic action needs prayer and prayer needs action. The 8th National Conference of the Catholic Layman's Retreat Movement was held from July 29–31, 1938, at Niagara University, New York. Attendance included 16 bishops, 25 monsignori, 100 priests, and 300 lay people. Delegates came from all across the United States and Canada. The Most Rev. John A. Duffy, the Bishop of Buffalo and the patron of the retreat, celebrated the opening Mass. Of interest are the papers and panels presented at the retreat:[12]

1. "The Day of Recollection"
2. "The Layman's Retreat Bulletin"
3. "Publicity for Retreats"
4. "Financing Nationally the Laymen's Retreat Movement"

The Mass featured Bishop James E. Kearney of Rochester. New York, preaching on Pius XI's encyclical *Mens Nostra* (December 20, 1929). The panels included the following areas:

1. "Developing a Successful Promoter"
2. "Promotion of Retreats on Parish and Diocesan Basis"
3. "The Laymen's Retreat and the Laboring Man"
4. "Practical Catholicism and Impractical Communism"

Business sessions and the banquet were held at the Hotel Statler in Buffalo, New York.

Locally, Fr. Pocock furthered the retreat movement by championing retreats at the London Holy Name First Diocesan Convention on November 15, 1938 in London, Ontario. "Rev. Dr. Philip Pocock" addressed

---

12 See "National Layman's Retreat Meeting," *The Catholic Record*, July 30, 1938, p. 1. The non-inclusive language is in these original articles, but men and women were definitely part of the movement.

300 delegates on the subject of "Retreats for Laymen." He indicated that the history and growth of the Movement had its real beginnings under Pope Pius XI "who wished to be known as the Pope of the Lay Retreat Movement." He lauded the development within the diocese of London and appealed to the Holy Name men to become "true apostles of this great work."[13]

Even young people were getting involved in making retreats in the diocese. The Youth Retreat Movement began in 1937 with four or five retreats given for children from local schools. Two years later, a Youth Retreat Movement Schedule was published indicating that these retreats now extended to forty parishes for children of local schools. It also indicated that retreats would be offered for children of upper classes in elementary schools, both public and Catholic, and especially for those children of parents who lacked employment. The retreats would be conducted exclusively by priests of the diocese who would volunteer their services, all under the directorship of "Rev. Dr. Philip Pocock, J.C.D., of St. Peter's Seminary." The schedule indicated the names of the priest-directors and the parishes where the retreats would be held.[14]

By the year 1939, the Laymen Retreat Movement was really picking up speed. Michael F. Walsh of New York, the U.S. Secretary of State, made a huge proposal in his speech at the 9th Conference of the Catholic Laymen's Retreat Movement in Brooklyn, N.Y. He recommended that a central organization be created to spread the retreat movement among American Catholics. His rationale for this is prescient for the call to holiness in our own diocese now: closed retreats are as old as Christianity itself; they are a tremendous factor in the spread and influence of Christianity; they enjoy Papal blessing and sanction; their survival is evident; they have a potential, immeasurable value to Church and Country, to family and individuals; and, they should be wisely and prudently propagated. He went on to indicate how a central bureau would be helpful for individual bishops and dioceses, that every diocese should have a "closed" retreat house with more than one in larger dioceses and archdioceses, and that there should be a retreat board in every parish within a radius of one hundred miles from the retreat house.

He revved up his enthusiasm for the national bureau with a battery of functions for it: arrange conversations about retreats; have discussions about the direction of retreats and their problems; provide conferences for retreat presidents and other retreat league officers; exchange ideas for other retreat expressions; transmit conclusions from these exchanges; publicize

---

13 "London Holy Name First Diocesan Convention," *The Catholic Record*, Nov. 26, 1938, p. 1.

14 See "Forty Retreats for Youth of London Diocese," *The Catholic Record*, Sept. 16, 1939, p. 1.

with propriety the retreat movement; help establish new retreat leagues; study promotional methods to break down the usual resistance for retreats; encourage fervor and perfection among the retreatants in making retreats; foster retreats for various classes of people, namely labourers, skilled mechanics, professional men, coloured (sic) Catholics and non-Catholics; win the favour and encouragement of pastors; and, make retreatans aware of local, national and international participation in a great Catholic activity. The great goal of the Retreat Movement was "a closed retreat house for men in every diocese, … a retreat for men from every parish and Catholic organization; and a strength born of unity to work for that goal."[15]

It is interesting to note how these promoters were trying, through retreats, to touch so many levels of Catholics, especially those who were disadvantaged by economic struggles, racial prejudice, and even non-Catholics. They were targeting men in particular, in an era when it may have been more difficult to get men to look more intensely into their spiritual well-being than women. (The Holy Name Society also had such a purpose.)

By 1940, it is evident that lay women were becoming very involved in making retreats. This is evident in an article entitled "Ottawa Laywomen Retreat Has Successful Year." It was a report of lay retreats in the Ottawa diocese for the Catholic Youth Organization (CYO), the Legion of Mary and Catholic Action groups. It mentioned the diocese's attendance at the 3rd National Laywomen's Retreat Congress in New York. Interestingly, Bishop John C. Cody, Ordinary of the Diocese of Victoria, B.C., was mentioned as being their spiritual director. Also, "A vote of thanks was passed on to the Rev. Dr. P.F. Pocock, London, Ontario, in appreciation of his valuable counsel on the work of closed retreats for youth and school-age groups."[16]

By now, the retreats for laymen were in full swing. The 5th Annual closed retreat of the London Laymen's Retreat Association was held at St. Peter's Seminary from August 30 to September 2, 1940. It was attended by seventy men, nearly all from London parishes and conducted by Fr. Athanasius Burke, C.P., of Dunkirk, N.Y. The London group was one of five units of the Diocesan Laymen's Retreat Association. In addition, five retreats were held that summer at the seminary, as well as one at St. Alphonsus Seminary, Woodstock, Ontario, the Redemptorist seminary.[17]

On June 29, 1944, Fr. Philip Pocock, the "founder of the Lay Retreat

---

15 "Would Put Laymen Retreat Movement on National Basis," *The Catholic Record*, Oct. 21, 1939, p. 8.
16 "Ottawa Laywomen Retreat Has Successful Year," *The Catholic Record*, Jan. 20, 1940, p. 5.
17 "London Laymen's Retreat Association" *The Catholic Record,* Sept. 14, 1940, p. 5.

organization in this diocese,"[18] was ordained Bishop of the diocese of Saska-toon at St. Peter's Cathedral in London. His successor as Director of the Retreat Movement in the Diocese of London was Fr. Arthur L. Meloche. This was a natural progression given his close personal proximity to the Pocock family while in the seminary and his assistance to Fr. Pocock in the retreat movement as a priest.

As World War II dragged on, the theme for the year's retreats was named: "Retreats for Peace." People were again urged to spend days in prayer and meditation on Christian truths, which constitute "the foundation of true and lasting peace." Retreats were also presented as an excellent preparation for those "preparing to play their part in the armed forces."[19] Dates were then given for summer retreats at the Seminary for French men; men of the Lon-don district; men of the Windsor district; and, at Brescia Hall for ladies (two retreats) and for business girls; and, finally, at St. Mary's Academy in Windsor for ladies and business girls (two retreats).

At this juncture, we must highlight another amazing development hap-pening concurrently with the retreat movement in this time period. Side by side on page 5 in the July 17, 1937 edition of *The Catholic Record* are two articles in an amazing juxtaposition: "Lay Retreats in London Diocese" and "Clergy Institute for Social Action." The latter article described a two-week summer course for the clergy of the London diocese held at the seminary in London and at Assumption College in Windsor, all under the auspices of Bishop Kidd. The sessions focused on a more thorough study of social mat-ters and prepared for an integrated study of social action at the diocesan level. Pope Pius XI's encyclical *Divini Redemptoris* (March 19, 1937) was the foun-dational document for this institute because it promoted an active lay aposto-late, studied social case work and institutional social planning. The institute studied the social encyclicals on wages, hours of labour and collective bar-gaining. It tried to implement what papal teaching was promoting: going to the working man, especially the poor; also, studying both the spiritual and material aspects of rural social life. The institute was conducted under Fr. J.A. Cook, M.A., a priest of the London diocese who was making a special study of these questions in Washington, D.C. It also indicated that a few priests from neighbouring dioceses followed these courses as well.

* * *

It is an old bromide that our spiritual life includes head, heart and feet. The brief outline of the development of the retreat movement in the London

---

18 "London Diocese Laity Retreat Dates Announced," *The Catholic Record*, June 24, 1944,
   p. 1.
19 *Ibid.*

diocese clearly manifests this truth. A wonderfully talented and academically competent individual in the seminary professor, Fr. Philip Pocock, spearheaded the retreat movement in our diocese. He was strongly led and supported by Bishop Kidd. However, it was the manifestation of the heartfelt need for quiet, spiritual renewal of both laymen and laywomen as well as of our bishops, priests and religious men and women. The final piece in our brief review shows how this spiritual renewal was accompanied by the concomitant development of studying and implementing the social teachings of the church, then, and perhaps even today, a largely hidden "secret" in the teachings of the church. Prayer without action can be simply dreaming; action without prayer can be only beating the wind. One needs the other for the gospel to be effective in any era.

Other interesting features of the retreat movement are worth reviewing here: the retreats were done both in some of our institutional settings as well as in the parishes; the parish priests often gave at least the one-day retreats in the parishes; the retreats expanded to include women, young people, various organizations, the poor, the racially marginalized, those in economic distress, people called to serve in the military, as well as priests and religious; the word "laity" replaces "laymen" and "laywomen." Other features include the value of total silence stressed along with a very structured format resembling that of seminary or religious order training; a high degree of collaboration between priests, religious and laity; a nascent ecumenical and interfaith openness to those who would want to make a retreat; and an involvement by the diocese in the broader unfolding of the retreat movement, both nationally and internationally.

We can also note the influence of St. Peter's Seminary faculty and venue as a kind of *leitmotif* through it all. This will continue in the ongoing development of the retreat movement in our diocese, as we shall see.

Affirmations

Time to leave. I got more from the weekend than I allowed myself to expect. It's always like that. If I allow it, life conspires to make me happy – and better – safe.

Affirmations

Aug. 22, 2008
Feast day of St. Monica

I've come to "THE OASIS,"

This room so aptly named.

Where, as at an oasis in the
desert.

Cooling refreshing waters for
a body thirsting so...

Here - it's waters of the
spirit restore

That cool my weathered soul

From the hot and sticky
journey

That seems to be our goal.

Here we find true meaning

As we prayerfully become
serene

And let go of earthly
pressures.

LET GO - LET GOD'S
creation be seen

For many times I've spent
here

As years have come and gone

My soul finds such
refreshment...

And not just mine alone

I pray to become a better
person

And take this home with me.

To spread God's gracious
blessing

For all the world to see.

Amen

Thanks be to God.

M.D.

Mar. 12/06
Inner Child Healing
Retreat

An Amazing experience; for
the first time I have allowed
myself to be in touch with
my "little girl." It has been
a fulfilling experience. I am
looking forward to meeting
her and discovering who she
really is - Thank You - ANN
+ the Holy Family Retreat!!
This is the only place I have
ever visited, where I have
felt so comfortable that I
allowed myself to bring down
my guard.

D.M.F.

St. Francis of Assisi
outside Nazareth House

chapter 2

The Founding of Holy Family Retreat House

T he Spirit began to move the laity for more retreat locations in the diocese. Once again, Sir Harry Gignac, accompanied by George and Armand Janisse, three of the key leaders of the professional group of men who attended the Cleveland retreats in the 1930s, went to see Bishop Kidd after the war to petition for a retreat house in Essex County. These men seemed to have been willing financially to help the diocese start up such a venture. Their plea fell on willing ears. During the 1946 retreats, Bishop Kidd formally announced to men on retreat his intention of building, not one, but two permanent, all-year-round retreat houses, one located in the Windsor district and the other in London. He indicated that gifts to the Diocesan Fund Campaign would be set aside for that purpose. Such retreat houses were seen as of utmost importance.

The search for a site began in earnest. They looked at different properties, one being the park in front of Assumption Church on the Detroit River. Another property they looked at was a large summer home on Lake Erie near Kingsville, which was later bought and occupied by the Sisters of St. Joseph as their summer home.

The house in front of St. Mary's Building before being bought by the diocese

The third one was a well-known roadhouse known as the Erie View Hotel located in the hamlet of Oxley on the shores of Lake Erie just east of Colchester. It was renowned for its cuisine and well known by the clergy (of course!). The property had six hundred feet of private beach and five acres of ground.[1] It had been operated for many years by Joseph and Catherine Malone, who were from Detroit, Michigan.

The main road in Oxley, c. 1920

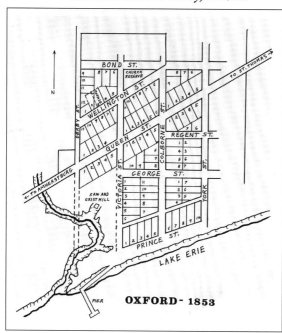

OXFORD - 1853

Oxford/Oxley Village

Let us pause for a moment to take a little historical peek at Oxley itself.[2] If we were to arrive there in 1853, it was a thriving little community called "Oxford." (See map.) It has a saw and grist mill, getting their power from a dam in the stream. The ravine is used to slide the logs down to the lake. Only in 1919 would they bridge the ravine for the road. It also enjoys a creamery, a lumber business, a grain warehouse and a post office. There is a well-known beach at the foot of Victoria Street.[3] Immediately to the west of Victoria Street is a laneway going down to a pier over 300 feet long, called Oxford Wharf. Fishermen bring in their catches to this pier, and logs are shipped out from there as well. Sand and gravel from the lakebed are hauled up the laneway, which would be known as

---

1   The original farm on "Lots 54 and 55" had been owned by Mr. and Mrs. George W. Sweeney. It was called "The Mill Property" as shown on Plan No. 188. See Diocesan Archives.

2   The material is from *Harrow and Colchester South 1792–1992*, Harrow, Ontario, Harrow History Book Committee, 1993, pp. 44; 118–119; 135–139; 164–165.

3   There was a set of 99 cement stairs (built in 1912) going down to the lake. It would be left unrepaired after the 1960s.

"Lovers' Lane" by 1924! As time passes, the beach would become well known to summer tourists, especially those from Detroit. The numerous homes in the area accommodate the many vacationers during the summer with lodging, meals, and hospitality. By the 1900s, there are two main hotels, the three-storey Ravine Hotel on the

The lane going down to the lake, called "Lovers' Lane" in 1924

west side of the ravine, and the Erie View Hotel nearer to the lake. A horse-drawn open bus brings in the tourists from Harrow, eight to ten at a time. Unfortunately, the village lacks boats for hire and a sports field.

By 1870, a Methodist church is on the east side of Victoria Street just opposite the Erie View Hotel, a beacon for sailors. But with the advent of automobiles, the hundreds of summer tourists become so disruptive of its afternoon Sunday services that it is forced to close in 1930. Remnants of its foundation remain

Oxley Beach, the Methodist church, and the cement staircase, c. 1925

to this day. Finally, the village came to be known as "Oxley" in 1883 because the post office felt that there were too many "Oxfords" in Ontario. Much of this village has now faded into non-existence so that sleepy, pastoral Oxley today doesn't even deserve a speed reduction on County Road #50 ... in many ways, ideal for a retreat setting.

Refurbishing the Erie View Hotel

Now, back to our story. The bishop contacted Fr. J.A. Roney and Fr. W. Langlois, and a few other priests, to investigate the feasibility of purchasing the Erie View Hotel. This happened just as the diocese was launching its first financial campaign in 1946 with one of its aims to provide money for a retreat house for the Windsor area. In 1947, the hotel buildings were purchased by the diocese "for a song" according to Fr. Ted Gatfield, a mere $38,000. Oral tradition maintains that Bishop Kidd, who had personally made the decision to buy the hotel, did so because it had good drinking water. (He was a plumber/farmer before being ordained.) "He never did leave the farm!" quipped Fr. Meloche.

Originally, there were only three buildings: the main building with kitchen, dining room and two more upper floors (now St. Mary's) with about

Holy Family Retreat House, c. 1960

ten rooms; a hotel dormitory building (where the present St. Joseph's Building is located), closer to the lake with about forty rooms and a large sun porch facing the lake which also served as a bookstore; and a house in front of the main building where the Malones lived. The location also had a waitress bunkhouse and a soda stand.

To remodel the hotel, Colonel Paul Poisson from Tecumseh recommended Armand Baillargeon and Sons to do the work. Mr. Baillargeon moved his family into the house on the property. Working at what was called a snail's pace, he managed to refurbish the dining room as well as the kitchen and some of the other buildings for $55,448.70. Fr. Meloche lived at St. Alphonsus parish in Windsor, and commuted back and forth to Oxley. He admits that he was not an administrator but more of a spiritual director. But everyone soon realized that something had to happen to speed up the work. Sir Harry Gignac and his cohorts galvanized the effort. These men of action fired the present carpenters, plumbers and electricians, and began the whole business of refurbishment with a new crew led by a certain Mr. Carl Sweet, who owned a construction company, telling them that it all had to be ready by the proposed grand opening of August 1, 1948. A man by the name of Mr. C.F. Petz was hired to install the plumbing and to keep the boilers steaming for the winter. The Baillargeons faded away.

Now things really moved along. The house was fully remodeled into a rectory for the retreat house director, Fr. Meloche, and the preachers chosen to conduct the retreats. The main building was soon completely refurbished and called St. Mary's Building. It contained seventeen private rooms, all reconditioned and equipped with running hot and cold water. Offices occupied some of the rooms on the second floor. The old dining room and kitchen were also completely renovated to meet the needs of the retreat house. The room just off the dining room, which was the reception room for the hotel, remained and was called "The Founder's Room." The women of the Catholic Women's League were invited to create curtains and make the various rooms more livable. Including a woman's touch was a deliberate indication that the retreat house was for both men and women.

Immediately to the west of St. Mary's Building is the Chapel of Christ the King. This is perhaps the most interesting piece of construction on the whole site. The sanctuary and the sacristy were part of a popstand from the former hotel. This was joined to the body of the chapel (formerly a bunkhouse where the maids used to stay). It was moved from down below where the statue of St. Francis is now, opposite Nazareth House. (It was not there as one of the original hotel buildings). The day before the opening of the retreat house, July 31, 1948, the little tower and bell were put on top of the chapel. The bell came from one of the old pioneer one-room schoolhouses in the area. Further renovations, as well as the beautiful carved wood frieze behind the altar and the other carved wooden statues, will be described later.

To the west of the chapel, the former hotel dormitory building was completely remodeled and dedicated to St. Joseph. Twenty-eight private rooms were equipped like those in St. Mary's Building. The extensive front lounge was maintained to provide an excellent view of Lake Erie. A wooded ravine borders the west side of the property.

A private space for parking was provided at the rear of the buildings. The whole cost of the remodeling was close to $152,000.[4]

Dedication of the Retreat House

At 3:15 p.m. on the Sunday afternoon of August 1, 1948, Bishop Kidd presided at the official opening ceremony on the front steps of the new chapel. Parish lay leaders were present for this event along with Fr. Meloche and the new board of twelve directors, six of them priests. Bishop Kidd's main message was that true Catholic Action insisted that lay people, who were now taking greater responsibility in the Catholic Church, needed a solid spiritual foundation. They needed training for this and so he called the retreat house a "Seminary for the Laity." He then went to each of the buildings to bless them with holy water. When he got to one of the buildings, Monseigneur Roney suggested that one "sprinkle" on the main floor would be adequate.

The opening ceremony of the Retreat House (1948)

The Bishop insisted that he go to every floor, because, as he said, "It *was* a road house, you know." A true pastor!

Bishop Kidd had insisted that there should be a group of men to take responsibility for the finances and ongoing remodelling of the hotel. The first board included some of the stalwarts who had been in the vanguard of the retreat movement in the diocese right from its conception:

- Rt. Rev. Wilfrid J. Langlois, D.P., Dean of Essex and Leo Page, honorary chairmen;

---

4   See Michael Power, Daniel Power, et al., *Gather up the Fragments – A History of the Diocese of London,* Published by the Diocese of London, Canada, 2008, p. 66–67.

- Sir Harry E. Gignac, K.S.G., chairman;
- Rev. J.A. Roney and Col. Paul Poisson, M.C., buildings and property managers;
- Rt. Rev. W. E. Dillon, D.P., and John Wall, financial committee;
- Rev. G.L. Blonde and George Janisse, organizational committee;
- Rev. I.J. Poisson and George Hanrahan, promotional committee;
- Fr. Arthur Meloche, Spiritual Director.

Fr. Meloche acted as secretary of the board, which had offices at Room 702, Canada Building, in Windsor, and at the retreat house. The jobs of janitor and housekeeper were given to Mr. and Mrs. Phil Denomme.

The Retreat House Starts to Grow

Fr. Meloche needed a chef. He discovered "Alex", a retired chef who lived in Windsor. He was hired for $50.00 a weekend to do the cooking. One of the main entrées on the Sunday night closing dinner was a turkey dinner. This was necessary because there were two or three turkey farms down the road that sold very inexpensive meat, thereby providing excellent turkey dinners. But "the trouble was that we had turkey on Sunday night and turkey stew and turkey salad and turkey, turkey, turkey for sixteen years. To this day, I don't eat much turkey!" opined Fr. Meloche.

What is his Greek last name?

The first spiritual event of the retreat house was a "closed" retreat for men from August 6–8, 1948. The Coadjutor Bishop of London, John C. Cody, was the first retreat master.

The retreat house needed a lively promotion. To this end, on the weekends Fr. Meloche would head off to the parish whose parishioners were on retreat at Oxley. He would preach at all the masses and then return to the retreat house for the closing. The pastor would come to give a closing talk to his people at the end of the retreat, a wonderful pastoral link for the spiritual growth of his people. Fr. Meloche also insisted that the retreats would be preached by "outside" preachers, even though he himself was a superb preacher. He wanted exciting and fresh material to inspire retreatants. He also insisted that, even though the retreat house was primarily for Catholics, anyone, regardless of creed, who wished to make a retreat, could do so at Oxley. He was a fore-runner of Vatican II.

We will pick up on the continued development and growth of the retreat house and the retreat movement as we examine in more detail various

Holy Family Retreat House, Oxley, Ontario,
November 3–7, 1948

directors of the retreat house. First steps had been taken. The site was secure and all kinds of individuals would soon feel a persuasive invitation to be supporters of Holy Family Retreat House under the very capable leadership of Fr. Meloche.

Affirmations

6-20-09

Today is the last day of my Kairos retreat. It has truly been a wonderful experience for me and for everyone here. Though it is my last day here in Oxley, Kairos will live in me for the rest of my life. The emotions I have felt, the friends I have made, and the experience I have been through are some that will always be with me as I walk through this life.

As for some words of wisdom to you. Your time here is very short. Enjoy the nature that is around you, chill with your friends that are with you, become close to those you are not close to, write stuff down, become one with the Lord, and live the fourth. Take your experiences with you back home. Don't be afraid to be open.

I am one of six Catholic Central guys to be sharing this experience with more than thirty U of D guys. I didn't know any of them coming to Kairos, but we are all leaving brothers. No one will judge you and they will all accept who you are. I think I've most of it, now go out and write in your journal, watch nature, or anything else here at Oxley.

I love you,

B.S.

Catholic Central 2010

Kairos LXVI

chapter 3

Fr. Art Meloche
"Determined Joy"

Director from 1948–1964

F r. Arthur Meloche grew up in Immaculate Conception parish in Windsor, Ontario. He was an only child whose parents had separated while he was in the seminary and so Fr. Phil Pocock took a personal interest in his needs. He became a part of the Pocock family who lived in London. As a seminarian, he used to help Fr. Pocock with the summer retreats given at the seminary before the retreat house opened.

He was ordained in 1941 and stationed at Immaculate Conception parish in Windsor, Ontario. Fr. Pocock asked him to be the director of the Windsor Men's Retreats. In 1944, when Fr. Pocock was appointed the Bishop of Saskatoon, Fr. Meloche was appointed the Diocesan Director of Retreats. He moved to St. Michael's parish in London to look after the development of the retreat movement for men and women in the diocese. Our previous chapter described his involvement in the founding of Holy Family Retreat House.

Fr. Meloche as a young priest

He died at Nazareth House, a retirement home for priests and laity in San Diego, California on May 21, 2008, after a brief illness. He was "only" 92 years old and sharp as a tack until the end. He left a remarkable legacy of experiences behind him. Fr. Ted Gatfield and I had flown down to visit him in August, prior to his death. We spent a week interviewing him as well as visiting several religious sites with him in the area. For me, it was the discovery of someone who truly lived the priesthood and life itself in high-definition colour.

Highly extroverted, gregarious, forceful, articulate, prayerful, a born communicator, even a bit of a "schmoozer," these are just a few descriptors of his qualities that impressed me. He had been a well-informed and highly influential preacher of the faith for over sixty years.

Sue Vetuschie, a dear long-time friend of Fr. Meloche, wrote a beautiful tribute for his funeral. She said that his homilies were engaging and always provided a very practical message for daily life. He was an avid reader and used the best of what he found in his readings from philosophers, psychologists and theologians to help translate the scriptures into very practical, human and inspirational terms. He may have come across to some as on the conservative side, but he had an amazing gift of surprising people with refreshing flashes of new insights and carefree, child-like demonstrations in song and actions.

He had a banner hanging in his room in San Diego which perhaps best epitomized his chief personal trait: *"Avec joie, je vous donne tout,"* roughly translated, "With joy, I give you my all." He loved the scene from the movie *The Bucket List* where it mentions an ancient Egyptian belief that everyone must answer only two questions before entering Heaven:

1.   Did you have joy in your own life?
2.   Did your life bring joy to others?

Joy was the centerpiece of his life. He lived giving joy in his vocation as a priest, as a friend, as a counselor, a listener, and even as a gin rummy player. His favorite description of joy—he maintained that it is different from happiness and other similar emotions—is the following list:

When you feel pleasure—you smile
When you feel glad, you might clap your hands
You feel merry when you have a couple of drinks
We say happy—when you begin anew—Happy New Year—Happy
Birthday
But joy is special—"It is the echo of God's presence within us."

Fr. Meloche had a zest for life. He preferred celebrating funerals to weddings, because you never know how the latter will turn out! In his residence in San Diego, he knew everyone by name, and readily communicated with them, even across the dining room while eating a meal. He insisted that he had celebrated Mass every day of his priesthood, and he also preached a punchy, pertinent homily each day for the residents. He was a priest through and through. This was the man we met in California.

The Growth of the Retreat House and the Retreats

Fr. Gatfield and I discovered a rich treasure-trove of information from Fr. Meloche as to how organization of the retreat house evolved. I will share these memories in a somewhat casual way so that we can experience a kind of "in-house," personal revelation of the gradual unfolding of Holy Family Retreat House from one of its Founding Fathers.

* * *

By 1950, the landscaping of the grounds began in full force. Fr. Meloche's sister, Mildred Reynolds, was a landscape architect who volunteered her services. They brought over $5,000 worth of evergreens from Toledo, Ohio, and planted them all around the property. Gradually, trees were planted along the road. Also, Larry Bondy erected a fence along Victoria Street. Very soon they realized they needed a caretaker to look after the grounds and maintain the buildings. Mr. Alex Petz and his wife took over the front house which Fr. Meloche used as a rectory. After a few years the renovators, Carl Sweet and Company managed to build on to St. Joseph's Building a beautiful knotty pine room, complete with fireplace, with a lovely view of Lake Erie, bedroom and bathroom—all connected with the suite that the Retreat Master used.

In all of this, he was blessed by a wonderful manager, Ella Oates. But soon they needed more help to run retreats as well as to maintain the grounds. Money was scarce. Who could help? Tradition prevailed. As in London, Fr. Meloche remembered his seminary assistance to Fr. Pocock for the summer retreats held there. A ready pool of willing seminarians was immediately available. Over the years, Joe Brisson, Gerry Freker, Willie Clark, Ted Gatfield, who was named the "assistant manager," Adrian Jansen, Gerry Langan, Larry Paré, Leo Reed-Lewis, Lionel Morand, Len Seguin, and a German seminarian (who only

Sir Harry Gignac and the seminarians

lasted one year) filled the support staff roster. They cleaned, painted, and worked on the grounds—they were available for just about everything. The roadhouse had a tennis court behind the main building. Needing more room for parking, the seminarians wielded sledge hammers to break up the concrete to make way for this necessity. Fr. Gatfield would further address parking needs when he became director. Of course, they had volunteered "gratis," or as Fr. Meloche put it— "for the greater honour and glory of God." Not surprisingly, most of these stalwarts were eventually either ordained as priests or became active Catholic laymen.

Fr. Meloche also remembers that Sir Harry Gignac and some of the men on retreat were there in the very first week for a day of recollection. However, they were afraid that someone would break into their cars in the parking lot. (Remember, they were "professional men.") So they hired some of the seminarians to watch their cars at night. One might wonder if the seminarians prayed Matins from the Breviary at 3:00 a.m. during their night vigil.

Very soon, Mr. Petz, their first engineer and a contractor from Tecumseh who had installed the heating and electrical systems, had run out of steam. Mr. Ted Boutette was hired as the new stationary engineer to handle the boilers. He had a family and so needed a place to live. A house named "Cana House"

Statue of the Holy Family next to chapel

Station donated by John Wall

was built on the highway for Ted and his family.

By 1956, some of the statuary on the grounds started to spring up. Dr. Beuglet, the father of Fr. Charlie Beuglet, who succeeded Fr. Gatfield at the retreat house, donated the statue of the Holy Family. All fourteen Stations of the Cross were donated, each costing $500.[1] Mr. Tony Collati donated the base for each station. More improvements came along: a landscaping and pumping scheme, parking lots, fences, outdoor lighting and a breakwater to help curb the cliff erosion from the Lake Erie waves. Placing cement crosses on the shoreline achieved this. Hefty donations, supplemented by help from Carl Sweet and his construction company, made a lot of this possible.

Nazareth House

The retreat house had blossomed since it opened in August 1948. The next year they had a total of 43 retreat events involving 1,863 retreatants. The average group attendance was 43. In 1956, they provided 62 retreats as well as five other groups. The total number of retreatants had almost tripled to 3,043 with an average attendance of 49.[2] They were paying all their bills, and had even started up a building fund. They

Nazareth House in 2008

realized there were no adequate accommodations for married couples. The retreats had been for women only, or for men only. What could be done?

A kind of "niche" was available on the property between St. Mary's Building and Victoria Street. In 1955, the architect J.C. Pennington prepared an original design for a two-story building to hold 54 private rooms. However, this had to be scaled down due to financial constraints. Hilliker and Crosby

1   See Appendix 1 for the names of these donors.
2   Their accountant, Francis S. "Stan" Arbour, has left us excellent annual financial statements, including the names of everyone employed each year, for the period of 1948–1960. He is to be commended for this remarkable feat of voluntary labour. We will not cite these names in detail, as we cannot do so for the other years of our inquiry. Someone would be left out for sure!

were hired as architects, and in 1956 the present Nazareth House sprang up to the east of St. Mary's Building. The general contractor was J.S. Thornton. It contained fourteen double rooms on one floor for use by married couples. Fr. Adrian Jansen wonders about one aspect of the rooms: "They had an interesting set up. There was a sliding door between two rooms and the hus-

*Statue outside
St. Mary's Building*

band was supposed to be in one room and the wife in the other. Why the sliding door, I have never been able to figure out. Maybe someone can explain this to me."[33] It also had a lounge at the south end of the building along with washrooms and showers for occupants.

It was built for $40,675 with money from their building fund, a donation from the diocese and a bank loan. It did not take long to pay off their deficit and to prepare for their next expansive move. Nazareth House was opened with an official blessing on September 11, 1957. However, it had already been used for the first retreat for married couples on August 3–5 of that year. A new dimension of "closed" retreats, sliding doors notwithstanding, was now in place. To top it up, Fr. Mike Dalton had a statue of Our Lady of Fatima and the visionaries behind his church in Kingsville. He decided to give them to Fr. Meloche and they were installed behind Nazareth House.

Indeed, the retreats' numbers continued for many years. To promote each retreat, Fr. Meloche would work the parishes in Essex and Kent County, speaking about four or five weeks before the date of that particular parish's retreat. Sometimes, they combined four or five parishes together for a retreat, but as the retreats grew in popularity, individual parishes would mount their own retreats.

Retreat "Organization"

The schedule resembled that of the seminary: morning prayer together in the chapel, enforced silence at all times except for an hour after supper, reading at meals, praying the rosary and doing the Stations of the Cross on the grounds. They rang the bell for morning prayers and for the Angelus, much to the annoyance of some neighbors. The stress on silence (a "closed" retreat) was key. Over and over again, Fr. Meloche stressed the importance of withdrawing from conversation in order to hear what God was saying to each retreatant.

---

3   Adrian Jansen, "St. Peter's Seminary and the Holy Family Retreat House: Another Vital Connection," *Alumni Bulletin*, no. 57 (December, 1997), pp. 34–36.

Most people coming from such a retreat felt quite proud that "they had kept the silence," something quite new for most lay people. Bishop Kidd would have been proud of his fledgling "Seminary of the Laity."

Fr. Meloche had his unique "commissioned officers" of "captains" and "lieutenants." These appointments were made on the retreat. He would interview these leaders about taking the position of organizing the retreat for the next year. While on their own retreat, he would call them into his room and ask them to take responsibility as a captain or lieutenant. Each lieutenant would be charged with trying to recruit ten retreatants. The captain was in charge of attracting at least fifty retreatants to fill the retreat house for a weekend. Even Jesus used a kind of military-like organization to divide up the five thousand people he would feed in the wilderness. Fr. Meloche knew his Master well.

Holy Family Retreat League

On file is the brochure of the Second Annual Banquet of the "Holy Family Retreat League," also identified as "La Ligue de la Retraite de la Sante Famille," held at the Prince Edward Hotel in Windsor on January 8, 1950. The toastmaster was George Hanrahan, a Windsor judge well known for his gentle disposition. Bishop Kidd said the prayer for His Holiness Pope Pius XII and Rt. Rev. Wilfrid J. Langlois toasted His Majesty King George VI. Sir Harry Gignac, K.S.G., gave the president's report and Col. Paul Poisson introduced the much beloved guest speaker, Most Rev. Charles L. Nelligan. Bishop John C. Cody made a few observations and Fr. Meloche gave acknowledgments. A wonderful line drawing of the retreat house facilities at that time graced the whole page. (See page 63.)

It is noteworthy to cite what is on the last page of the brochure:

HOLY FAMILY RETREAT LEAGUE AND CATHOLIC ACTION

Following the Papal program for Catholic Action, Holy Family Retreat League bases its organization on two convictions:

1. Under the direction of our Bishops and with close co-operation of our parish priests, Holy Family Retreat League sponsors the Lay Retreat Movement for the laity of the Diocese of London.
2. Since the parish is the basic unit of the organization of Holy Mother Church, retreat groups, where possible, centre on the parish. Holy Family Retreat League has as its main objective to assist the parish priests in the spiritual formation of lay apostles.

front row: Bishop Cody, Bishop Kidd, Bishop Nelligan;
back row: Sir Harry Gignac, Fr. Meloche, George Hanrahan

...and they all had a
brief (?) speech!

This is all repeated in French on the same page. Again, we see the fundamental conviction that Catholic action must be rooted in prayer and spiritual formation. It also implies that usually prayer and spiritual formation must have an outward thrust through some kind of apostolic activity. Prayer without works can be flighty and works without prayer can be fruitless. Also evident in this description is the close relationship of the clergy, parishes and the laity. The league sponsored about six retreats a year, and only for lay *men*. It was a powerful testimony of efforts to get these men, perhaps not especially noteworthy for their religious fervor in those days, to take responsibility for deepening their spiritual lives. Of course, the retreat house had retreats for lay women as well, so there was no intent to exclude. Men just seemed to demand a bit more organizing and support.

Financial Survival

How did the retreat house survive financially? The initial cost of purchasing property and renovating buildings was mostly borne by the diocese, assisted by donations from "The Founding Fathers." They soon realized that some facilities needed improvement. In the early 1950s, $14, 418 was spent on the caretaker's house, $6,493 for the addition of priest's quarters in St. Joseph's Building, and $4,771 to enlarge the kitchen in St. Mary's Building. They also managed to buy a 1956 Dodge Crusader for $2,686, a 1949 Ford Pickup for $1,525 and a 1954 Plymouth Suburban for $2,475. Mobility was essential with the seemingly remote location of the retreat house.

After these initial financial jump-starts from the diocese, they were on their own. At first, they suggested a fee of $10 per retreatant for a weekend. This proved to be insufficient. Stan Arbor was their financial chairman, working out of his own house and using a Knights of Columbus office in Windsor. He used to come in at each retreat, record their financial statement, look over their costs, and see what they took in. His annual reports, housed in the diocesan archives, are an outstanding tribute to good financial reckoning. On Saturday evenings, after speaking in the parish, Fr. Meloche would return to Oxley and speak to retreatants about retreat costs. He indicated that they did not force anyone to pay, but he was clear about actual expenses. No one knew how much each person gave, as each retreatant simply handed in an envelope at the offertory at Mass. Gradually, they had to suggest $12, then $15, and then $17 for a long time. The method worked. They met expenses.

Other contributions included the famous $1.00 bill with the image of King George VI, sent in by Mr. Daniel Kearns from Electric, Ontario, a small community near Wallaceburg. It is framed in the present dining room with a very touching accompanying letter. Like the widow's mite in scripture, grati-

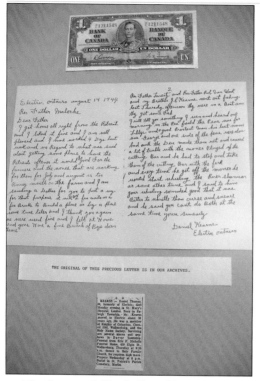

The famous dollar bill and letter in the dining room at St. Mary's Building

tude knew no limits of either education or amounts.

Dr. Paul Poisson donated $500 a year for the books needed in the chapel and for the library. Fr. Meloche was able to buy all the books he wanted to read, and so he kept up in spiritual reading. With no assistance from the diocese, financial assistance for the retreat house was requested from other diocesan bishops. Response: $00. Undaunted, Fr. Meloche even went on CKLW radio for about ten years to promote retreats. All these efforts were so successful that by the time he left the retreat house, there was no less than $120,000 in the bank which he hoped would provide for a new chapel. That was not to be, as we will see.

Help from Religious Women and Others

Help was needed to do the cleaning. At first, some women from Harrow came out to clean before and after each retreat. This was quite an expense, so Fr. Meloche asked Bishop Kidd to write to Rev. Mother M. Ignatius at Bethany Motherhouse in Antigonish, N.S., seeking help. The letter went out on January 30, 1950. She agreed to send some sisters to take over the domestic work. But just before they were set to come, they had to cancel.

With his usual doggedness, Fr. Meloche now went to the Religious Hospitallars of St. Joseph from Hôtel-Dieu Hospital in Windsor, Ontario. His request fell on willing ears. Sr. Marie de la Ferre, Sr. Claire Antaya, Sr. Marentette and Sr. Ruth Jeanette were the first religious sisters to wind their way on Walker Road to the lake to help out for the first retreat. They were not only helpful but continued to do yeoman work. They brought sheets, pillowcases, towels, washcloths and even some of the food, such as vegetables, from the hospital. Moreover, they provided a cook, Leonard Bertelli, and some of their kitchen staff as well. On Sunday evening, they took the laundry from the weekend back to the hospital for washing and then brought it all out on the following Friday for the next retreat. Could the CEO of a modern hospital ever allow this today?

Some of the other sisters from the hospital who helped during their three years at Oxley were Sr. Viola Beaulieu, Sr. Corinne Monforton, Sr. Bernadette Gouin, Sr. Aurore Beaulieu, and Sr. Eva Papineau. The sisters even donated linens, housekeeping items, chairs, and small desks with three shelves on each side. Needless to say, the sisters also offered many prayers for the retreatants along with their labours. The loving generosity of these remarkable religious sisters in Essex County was boundless.

However, Hôtel-Dieu Hospital needed the sisters full time, so they had to serve notice to Fr. Meloche. Desperate once again, he put out a plea to all the religious communities for help. No immediate response. Then Mother Margaret, the Superior-General of the Sisters of St. Joseph in London, Ontario rang in.[4] With the approval of Bishop Cody, she sent three sisters for a period of seven years. They were actually there from 1950–1959. Sr. Francis Joseph Kennedy, Sr. Thecla Martens and Sr. Marie (Rufina) Laprise brought their cooking and baking skills, much to the delight of the seminarians (naturally!). Fr. Meloche moved out of his residence to an apartment in the former St. Joseph's Building to accommodate them. The Sisters also made many financial donations each year to support the retreat house.

The work was hard, but they were young, strong and

Sr. Rufina (Marie) Laprise, Sr. Francis Joseph Kennedy, Fr. Meloche, Cardinal Léger, Bishop Cody, Sr. Carmela Reedy

Sr. Thecla Martens, C.S.J., and Sr. Marie (Rufina) Laprise, C.S.J.

4   Some of this section is from a small brochure of the Sisters of St. Joseph, London, Ontario, "Remembrances of Holy Family Retreat House," from the Archives of Mount St. Joseph, Courtesy of Sister Pauline Leblanc.

laughed a lot. Mrs. Stollar, a woman from Harrow, came to help with the cooking for a year. Then they discovered Mrs. Theresa Egervari who spoke very little English and knew nothing about Canadian cooking. Generous, a quick learner, she quickly got up to speed. She would go to different farms to pick up fruits and vegetables before she came to work, even on her time off, thereby saving the retreat house a lot of money. Everyone remembers her cheerful disposition, but especially how she could instantly dispel even the most rigid diet with her delectable cooking.

The sisters also took care of the sleeping quarters, chapel and the retreat master's quarters. For a period of time Sr. Jacinta Macinnis, Sr. Carmella Reedy and Sr. Virginia Lobban replaced Sr. Francis Joseph and Sr. Thecla. Sr. Antonia Gignac was Fr. Meloche's secretary from 1954–1955, to be succeeded by Lila Doyle from Harrow, who did this for more than twenty years.

In those days they did not have cars and there were neither buses nor trains in the surrounding area to take them anywhere. They were pretty well confined to the retreat house property. Occasionally, their generous weekend helpers, business girls and students from Windsor and immediate areas, would offer to take them to St. Joseph's Convent in Windsor on their return

home after the retreat. The sisters all remember how delightful it was to have these girls around to help them out. And, all for *gratis*, or "for the glory of God," to quote Fr. Meloche.

Eventually, the Sisters of St. Joseph had to leave and once again Fr. Meloche was in desperation-mode.

Theresa Egervari and Joanna Franco

An amazing series of events took place in 1959. Fr. Patrick Peyton was preaching on the Family Rosary Crusade in the London diocese at St. Mary's parish in London. He met Bishop Cody who shared with him his need for a group to staff the diocesan retreat house since the Sisters were leaving. Father Peyton indicated to him that he knew of a Secular Institute in Spain with great experience in the work of retreat houses. Bishop Cody, who had to go to Rome for his Ad Limina visit, stopped in Spain to meet the Director General and Co-Founder of the Institute of Secular Missionaries (ISM). They discussed the possibilities of accepting the invitation and finally it was decided to ask five ISM members if they would agree to come to Canada. Those five members, Angela Aisa, Maria

Teresa Bianchi, Julia Bellord, Araceli Echebarria and Margarita Arigoyen arrived at Oxley in October of 1959.[5]

I cannot resist telling the same story from the "oral tradition of Fr. Meloche" as told to Fr. Gatfield and myself in California. One night, at precisely 3:00 a.m. (he says!), he was suddenly awakened by a phone call from Fr. Patrick Peyton, the priest who inspired so many people in our diocese to pray the family rosary in the 1940s and 50s. He had met him when he gave a talk at St. Mary's parish in London where Fr. Meloche was an assistant. He was calling *from Spain (!)* where he was making some movies for his rosary crusade. He had heard that Fr. Meloche needed some sisters to help at Oxley. Indeed, he had discovered some members of The Institute of Secular Missionaries, with a charism for working in retreat work, who seemed in search of a new missionary experience. Few people even knew what a Secular Institute was in those days. Characteristically, Fr. Meloche's instinctive response was pithy and decisive:

"Pat, it's three o'clock in the morning in the middle of the night!"

"Oh, I understand you're looking for nuns to help at the retreat house. We've got these secular missionaries and they are willing to come. How many would you like to have?"

"We'll have them. Send over five of them!"

"Good night!"

Of course, the bishop had approved their coming and Msgr. Roney wrote out a cheque for $1,237.07 to cover their travel expenses. For the next thirty years, their help was inestimable. In spite of their difficulties with the English language, they very quickly adapted to the Canadian culture. They served as housekeepers, secretaries, receptionists and remarkable bearers of hospitality. They were remarkable consecrated women of deep prayer lives. They dressed simply but elegantly. Everyone remembers how willing they were to undertake the smallest task, doing even that with dignity. They could laugh at their own foibles as they learned English and discovered how to eat corn *off* the cob with one's fingers. They very quickly ingratiated themselves with the clergy and laity of the diocese. Fr. Meloche beamed. Once again, God had provided.

More Developments

We must also pay tribute to the countless lay men and women who served on various boards and support groups for the retreat house. Names like Irene

---

5   I am indebted to Ruth Beitia and some other members of the Institute of Secular Missionaries still here in Canada who met and provided me with the exact details of how they came here. See page 59 for a picture of some of them.

Page and Leo Page deserve specific mention. Armand Janisse, a board member, would drive out on Sunday evenings to be at the closing dinner for each retreat. The Holy Family Founders' Club provided much solid spiritual and financial support for the retreat house. Many of these men belonged to the Knights of Columbus.[6] It is remarkable how vital the retreat house was in nourishing their spiritual lives.

International Connections

Fr. Meloche had an innate ability to learn from others. He admitted that he had no idea how to organize retreats when he first started out. So early on, he and Sir

Fr. Meloche's famous booklet

Harry Gignac attended the National Catholic Women's Retreat Conference held in St. Louis, Mo. Hector Lucier, the owner of Lucier Drainage, a big construction owner from McGregor, Ontario, paid Fr. Meloche's way. Their main purpose was knowing how to fill a retreat house with retreatants, a timeless challenge. They listened to a Fr. "Ciumenato," S.J., who ran one of the most successful retreat houses in the United States. There they learned how to build a retreat house. He also got the idea from this dynamic Jesuit to prepare a small prayer book, 15–20 pages long, to give to each retreatant. He subsequently expanded and published this book.[7] Fr. Meloche checked out the Passionist Retreat House in New York and the retreat director there gave him all kinds of new ideas. Other venues for this conference included one at St. Anne's parish in Detroit which also accommodated the proximate Windsor connection, thereby allowing other Canadians easy access. In all these encounters, his powerful personality enabled him to be elected as the National Moderator of the Retreat Movement, a post he held for six years. He was the only Canadian on the committee. Bishop John Wright of Pittsburgh was the episcopal moderator.

One of the biggest events of the year was the annual banquet in Windsor

---

6   See Appendix 1 for a detailed list of all those involved in the original organization of the retreat house see the *Knights of Columbus Bulletin*, Vol. 25, January, 1949.

7   A.L. Meloche, ed., *A Souvenir of my retreat at Holy Family Retreat House*, Oxley, Ontario, 72 pp.

held around the first part of the year. Big-name speakers were invited including Paul Martin, Sr., the ubiquitous, long-time Liberal M.P. for Essex, and Bishop Emmett Carter, London's auxiliary bishop living in Windsor. Four to five hundred people came from all over Essex and Kent County. In 1964, about 1,500 people from Canada and the United States attended

Bishop John Wright at a retreat movement convention

the first International Lay Retreat Conference outdoor Mass at the University of Windsor. Six bishops participated: Coadjutor Archbishop P.F. Pocock of Toronto, Archbishop George Flahiff of Winnipeg, Archbishop John F. Dearden of Detroit, Bishop G. Emmett Carter, Bishop C. L. Nelligan of Assumption University and Bishop John J. Wright of Pittsburgh, Pennsylvania. No lack of episcopal support here!

Fr. Meloche was determined to be *au courant* for the needs of married men and women. He became involved in the

Six Bishops at Lay Retreat Conference

About 1,500 persons from Canada and the United States attended the first International Lay Retreat Conference highlighted the conference held in Windsor and Detroit. Celebrant was Archbishop John F. Dearden of Detroit. Bishop G. Emmett Carter of London delivered the sermon.

Pictured above are the six bishops who participated in the Mass. From left, Coadjutor Archbishop P. F. Pocock of Toronto; Archbishop George Flahiff of Winnipeg; Archbishop Dearden; Bishop Carter; Bishop C. L. Nelligan of Assumption University, Windsor; and Bishop John J. Wright of Pittsburgh, Pa.

(left to right) Bishop Pocock, Archbishop Flahiff,
Archbishop Dearden, Bishop Carter,
Bishop Nelligan, Bishop Wright

Family Life Program, even attending some of their conferences in Chicago where he listened to Msgr. George Egan. A national Cana Study Week was held July 12–15, 1954, at the retreat house. He was instrumental in forming a Family Life Bureau in the London diocese. Elsewhere, his fame led him to be selected as the only Canadian on the Family Life Bureau in Washington. He

BACK TO SCHOOL — Windsor police began a refresher training course Monday at the Windsor police department. The eight-week course will be attended by all officers from cadets to sergeants under the direction of Deputy Chief John Burns and Sgt.-Maj. Charles Weston. Each officer will take a week's training course during the eight weeks. Capt. A. L. Meloche, police chaplain, is seen instructing one class. *(Star Staff Photo)*

Fr. Art Meloche in action

Fr. Meloche at Archbishop Antonucci's Oxley visit

Fr. Meloche and a group of retreat directors in conference

also brought in other renowned speakers such as Fr. Clem Kern, the "Conscience of Detroit," for a three-day retreat life.

Fr. Meloche was determined to be involved in his community. By 1964, he was the chaplain for the Windsor Police Department, even giving instructions to police officers. They probably heard more than how to catch a thief, but rather how to help him repent and make a retreat at Oxley.

Holy Family Retreat House thrived on a cross-fertilization of ideas. Protestant and Jewish speakers, as well as many speakers of different backgrounds, would come to the airport in Detroit, be driven to Windsor and speak to the priests of the diocese. Everyone liked to come to Oxley because it was inexpensive. Fr. Meloche also got to know the head of the Detroit branch of Alcoholics Anonymous (AA). He was invited to come to Oxley for a retreat. He not only filled the place but even added some extra money to the hungry coffers of the retreat house. Ongoing retreats for AA individuals became a staple for the retreat house, even to this day.

Preaching Retreats in the United States

By 1964, Fr. Meloche was in need of a rest. He was more and more in demand to preach retreats in the United States: Ohio, Michigan, Wisconsin, Minnesota, North Dakota, Montana, Washington, Oregon, Alabama, Florida, and even in the Bahamas. He found this work thrilling. He was in love with giving retreats. In

More happy retreat directors in the USA

1965, he decided to spend a year in Paris and Rome studying the changes in the church following Vatican Council II with some of those who were instrumental in making these changes. In an interview a few years later, he described how he used this knowledge in talking with older priests who may be "on the defensive with regard to new approaches they didn't understand."[8] With younger priests, he tried to help them to understand the value of the older traditions which they wanted to reject. He looked back on his 25 years of preaching retreats and the considerable development in retreats since the days when they had the traditional format stressing the necessity of silence and the individual approach to God. He mused: "Since Vatican II, the big emphasis has been on the concept of the church as community, and of the necessity not only of listening to God in silence and contemplation, but listening to God speaking through one's neighbor."

He continued by explaining how the "dialogue" retreat first became popular about five or six years ago, but more recently there has been a swing back toward a "balance" of both silent retreats and discussion. He stressed that at certain stages of our lives, maybe one way is more beneficial than another. Whatever the format, the message being stressed is the community — the church as a community of people who are growing in believing, hoping and loving — timeless wisdom.

In 1964, Fr. Ted Gatfield was appointed by Bishop Carter as "rector" of the retreat house. On returning to Canada, Fr. Meloche was assigned as pastor of St. Mary's church in London, Ontario but this was clearly not enough for his towering preaching energies.

An invitation from his friend Bishop Wright to come and preach retreats

8   Mary Trueman, "Retreats his forte," *The Windsor Star*, April 8, 1972, p. 18. The rest of this post-Vatican II period of his life is drawn from this article.

in the United States would lure him away from the diocese. Bishop Carter gave his permission "for a year" and the rest is history. He never came back to live in Canada. In his first year away, he gave no less than forty-five retreats to deacons, sisters, and married couples. His "call within a call" blossomed.

A Retreat Director for All Seasons

Fr. Meloche had truly run with the ball handed to him by Fr. Philip Pocock. The retreat house and its reputation was firmly established when he took his leave. He was now launched into a kind of "second career" in the retreat movement with his work in the United States. Some might think that his

departure from the diocese was due to the inevitable clashing of two Titans, Bishop Emmett Carter and himself. Yet, no one doubts that Fr. Meloche had set some powerful currents flowing in Oxley: providing a prayerful venue for spiritual renewal for Catholic men and women, other people of all religious denominations, and professionals and non-professionals; a collaborative administration model that included religious women, lay people, seminarians, as well as local priests and parishes; a venue for spiritual

'Early' Fr. Meloche in the director's suite in the old St. Joseph's Building.

renewal for people suffering from addictions like alcohol; a connection with the international retreat movement in the United States plus with all kinds of leaders of current theological directions; and a focus for the fledgling Catholic Family Movement and the need to encourage sexual education for children by their parents.

His legacy to the retreat movement in the London diocese can perhaps best be described by a beautiful reflection done by Sr. Marie (Rufina) Laprise, C.S.J., one of the valiant religious mentioned earlier who worked at Oxley:

"Some of my happy memories of Oxley are going to sleep at night to the sound of waves lapping on the shore of the lake, and when we were alone there was nothing better than having early breakfast out on the lawn listening to the songbirds and watching the boats on the water.

Having the privilege of our own private Chapel gave us the opportunity of making many visits to the Blessed Sacrament. Our retreat days were special. We often made many holy hours for the intentions recommended to our prayers.

I praise God for the number of dedicated souls who have consecrated their lives to God as a result of contacts with the retreat house. I praise Him too, for using us as instruments of reconciliation. Recently, I returned to Oxley for a retreat and I cannot express the reverence I experienced for that holy and lovely place. I found there the same spirit of friendliness and hospitality that existed many years ago.

Blessed be God."[9]

Her tribute is a wonderful summary of Fr. Meloche's legacy to the retreat movement in our diocese, and to the value of making a retreat with a high degree of prayerful silence. The man of "Determined Joy" had launched it all. Not bad for someone who "had no gifts for administration!"

---

9   See note 4 above.

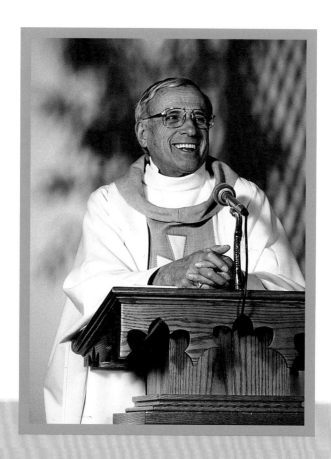

chapter 4

Fr. Ted Gatfield
"Reflective Gentleness"

Director from 1964–1969

I n 1939, Canada entered World War II while Fr. Gatfield was attend- ing Assumption College in Windsor, Ontario. He had completed two years of engineering when he decided to join the Royal Canadian Air Force. He later graduated as a pilot. While flying to San Diego to visit Fr. Meloche in 2007, I asked him what was the most difficult part of flying. His response was subtle: "Mickey, do you realize the world is a ball. Did you ever try landing on a ball?"[1] With such a reflective and engaging kind of humour, I looked forward to discovering more about him as well as Fr. Meloche along with new developments at the retreat house. I was not disappointed.

Our week together revealed to me someone who is gentle, kind and, in spite of failing eyesight, does not miss anything. He has a keen interest in just about everything. He loves people and moves easily in any kind of company, professional or ordinary folk. He has a deep trust in the providence of God, and this was manifested in some of his darkest hours in his vocation as a priest. He is full of wonder and awe. He is grateful for whatever God sends his way in life, trying as this can be at times. Truly, he is a good priest who deeply loves God and all the people he has served in his active ministry.

Born on October 4, 1921, he grew up in Amherstburg, Ontario, in a solid stone house almost next to the historic Fort Malden. After joining the Air Force, he was assigned to be a bomber pilot and to join the Japanese theater of war. This was not to happen. In 1945, the atomic bomb abruptly and devastat- ingly ended the war in the Pacific. As a result, many of the military from the war returned to university. By 1947, he had managed to graduate with a

---

1   Much of this chapter is taken from oral and written submissions from Fr. Gatfield, includ- ing a file of his on his time at the retreat house, which is housed at the London diocesan archives.

Bachelor of Arts degree from the University of Western Ontario in London through its affiliate, Assumption College, in Windsor. As well as studying, he and Norm Harrison managed to form Harrison and Gatfield Photographers with their names appearing on many outstanding pictures and portraits. But God had other plans for him.

Neither engineering nor photography could satisfy him. He became restless and sought advice from Fr. Meloche, who had been assigned in 1947 to set up the retreat house in Oxley. He suggested that he join him in this adventure as an "assistant," or "joe boy" as he said. This proved to be a wonderful experience for him.

Fr. Meloche was "God" to him, firing up a young Ted full steam ahead toward a new career and vocation that he began to love; he was being groomed for the seminary. Every day Fr. Meloche rang the bell for lunch. There was no dilly-dallying. His prayer life and love of God expanded in this context. His good friend, Wilfrid "Willy" Clarke of Harrow, had similar aspirations. They had come on board at the retreat house along with three sisters from Mount St. Joseph mentioned earlier. Other seminarians like Larry Paré joined them later during the six summers they spent at the retreat house. They prayed together, worked together and became friends. Numerous jobs abounded as they prepared for the retreatants who were now coming in great numbers each weekend. Seventy-five beds demanded frequent changing. They took the laundry to Ouellette's Laundry in Kingsville. With some exaggeration, Fr. Gatfield thinks they served about "one thousand meals" a week, doing everything from peeling potatoes to washing dishes.

One job was to break up the old tennis courts behind the former roadhouse to make room for the Stations of the Cross. These stones became part of the wall on the west side of Nazareth House. They also built the retaining cement wall behind St. Mary's Building to keep it from sliding into the ravine. They helped to position on the grounds a statue of Our Blessed Mother donated by Fr. Mike Dalton. They were especially proud of their work in planting and attending to the landscaping and greenery for the whole site. Fr. Meloche's sister, Mildred Reynolds, a professional landscape architect, tutored them in this satisfying work. They became strong, healthy young men, blossoming both physically and spiritually. The results of their labours are clearly manifest today, providing a lush, verdant setting for the retreatants' prayer and meditations.

In September, 1949, they both entered St. Peter's Seminary. One of the tasks during those fruitful summers for Willy and himself at Oxley was to paint the wooden picket fence along their property on Victoria Street leading to the lake. The painting was endless, simply because Fr. Gatfield made a huge discovery which he told me: "Did you know that a wooden fence has *four* sides?" This is a lesson many student painters learn very painfully to this day. Their one constant consolation were the warm tarts which the sisters often emptingly placed on the kitchen window sill. However, for Fr. Gatfield the whole experience of working at the retreat house was "all about learning about God's world." True "retreat attitudes" were already seeping into him. Fr. Meloche and the sisters loved the seminarians dearly and possibly spoiled them as well. It was all a valuable part of the grand preparation for their ordination on June 4, 1955 at St. Peter's Cathedral in London.

Another Diocesan Retreat House?

Along with his first parish assignments at St. Michael parish and Holy Cross parish in London, Fr. Gatfield was asked by the bishop to succeed two priests looking after the retreats in London: Fr. Frank Loebach, the seminary successor of now-bishop Pocock, who looked after the laymen's retreats at St. Peter's Seminary, and Msgr. John O'Donnell who organized the laywomen's retreats at Brescia Hall. Over three hundred women made six annual retreats at Brescia Hall in the summer under the hospitality of the Ursuline Sisters. Probably the same number did so at the seminary.

But now, episcopal inspiration was again at work. At this time, Bishop Cody felt that there should be at least another retreat house in the northern part of the diocese in the London area. He asked Fr. Gatfield to spearhead this possibility. Accordingly, Fr. Gatfield set up a Board of Directors of lay people, which included people like Jack Adams, and George and Mary McEvenue. They held their first meeting at the Hotel London, along with the bishop and other outstanding lay Catholics of the area. In their search for a site, they dis-

covered some beautiful land in the Grand Bend area near St. Peter's Church in St. Joseph, Ontario. This would have been a solid historical and holy root for a retreat house. Today, a cairn standing at the intersection of highways 21 and 84 indicates that newly canonized St. André Bessette

The main building at the Retreat House at Port Burwell

used to vacation there. He was the saintly religious Brother whose healing miracles made him famous in Canada and who instigated the building of St Joseph's Oratory in Montreal.

But then came a surprise. A wealthy Catholic layman, Gerry Livingstone offered his estate in Port Burwell for a retreat site. Everyone on the board was delighted. But this joy did not last long. The diocesan chancellor, Fr. Fergus Laverty, refused to accept the property due to the stipulations regarding a five year tax rebate. Some time later, the Passionist Fathers felt they could abide by these conditions, and the Port Burwell Retreat House was born.

Bishop Carter, the auxiliary bishop of London, succeeded Bishop Cody who died on December 5, 1963. In true Carter form, he made an indelible episcopal proclamation in his opening address in St. Peter's Cathedral which is deeply embedded in our diocesan corporate memory: "Bishop Fallon is dead! Bishop Kidd is dead! Bishop Cody is dead! I am the bishop." Fr. Gatfield heard these cannon-like outbursts, and being one of Bishop Cody's men, immediately thought: "and Fr. Gatfield is dead!" He felt his dream, and Bishop Cody's as well, for another retreat house was now history. Bishop Carter soon replaced most of the key people in responsible positions such as the seminary rector, Msgr. A.P. Mahoney, and the chancellor Msgr. A. Roney. But, deep down, Fr. Gatfield wondered, "What does God want?"

"Rector" of Holy Family Retreat House

About this time, Fr. Meloche was indicating that he needed a rest and wanted to get away. In keeping with his replacement spirit, in 1965, Bishop Carter appointed Fr. Gatfield the "rector" of Holy Family Retreat House, Oxley.

Tempestuous times were now tormenting the church. Vatican II ended in 1965. A wave of enthusiasm swept over much of the church, but many of its undigested teachings wreaked havoc on the faith-practice of Catholic priests and laity alike. Fr. Gatfield remembers how statues of saints were stripped from churches and stashed in cold basements or garages, altars were turned around, Mass was now celebrated facing the people, and Latin training for altar servers seemed at an end. These were only a few of the many changes that were implemented with an often-inadequate catechesis. Not surprising, the people coming on retreat were confused, upset, and angry about what was happening in their

parishes. Fr. Gatfield tried to provide a solid battery of people who were considered good preachers to implement Vatican II. These included members of the Redemptorist order such as the Grannon brothers, Fr. Eddie Boyce, and the de Monfortain Fathers such as Fr. Gerry Pocock.

The staff at the retreat house somehow managed to keep their cool in this roiling tempest. An attractive brochure published in 1967 gives a grand summary of what was happening at the retreat house. Fr. Gatfield is now listed as the "Director." Mr. E.J. Boutette was the Engineer and Mr. Anton Frank was on maintenance. The members of the Lay Institute were Nora Aragones, Ruth Beitia, Christine Serrano, Araceli Echebarria, and Julia Zalbidea. Mrs. Theresa Egervari is listed as a kitchen assistant. Then follows a complete list of the officers of the Holy Family Retreat League including Joseph L. Johns, Past President; Hector Lucier, President; Alice Serneels, Secretary; M. Frank Probst, Finance; Richard J. Bondy, Constitution; Vincent G. Janisse, Founders' Club; Raymond Lyons, Planning and Promotion; Charles Gress, Building Committee; Frank Morris, Public Relations; Edward Carson, Property and Maintenance; Beatrice Jobagy, Organization Women; and Paul Maitre, Organization Men.

The next six panels of the brochure contain a hugely impressive list of all the retreats scheduled for the year. It deserves being detailed: students, married couples, Regis Clubs of the diocese, Y.C.W. and University Students, Boys of all

Margaret Arigoien (left); Araceli Echebarria (right); Nora Aragones (back left); Julia Zalbidea (right); Ruth Beitia (center)

For contents of this brochure, see Appendix 4.

Parishes (Age 16 to 18), Girls of all Parishes (Age 16 to 18), Men, Women Engaged Couples, Retreat for A.A., Ladies of all Parishes, Priests, Grade 8 Days of Renewal, Les Dames Hors de la Ville de Windsor, Les Dames de la Ville de Windsor, St. Vincent de Paul Society, Legion of Mary, Summer Institute for Priests, Men—Labour Day Retreat, Study Day for Religious Superiors, Brennan High School, Business Women, Student Nurses of Chatham Dairymen, Renewal Days for Teachers, Les Hommes de Windsor et de L'Ouest du Compte D'Essex, Students, University of Detroit Boys, Les Hommes du Compte de Kent et de L'Est du Compte D'Essex, and Les Jeunes Filles qui Travaillent.

The brochure also lists the names, *and even phone numbers,* of specific local priests, called "Chaplains," and various "Organizers" and "Leaders" for the 106 different groups coming to Oxley that year. The files reveal that some 4,040 individuals came that year, donating $55,368.00. In one simple publication, we have a snapshot of the lay retreat movement in this end of the diocese, showing a remarkable amount of organization and participation of hundreds of individuals.

In addition, Lila Doyle continued to lend a hand at things. All kinds of volunteers and high school students kept coming out on weekends to do the necessary serving work. Jim and Barbara Kurtz helped on the Board. People were clearly being fed spiritually and materially at Oxley.

None of this was easy on the gentle and peace-loving Fr. Gatfield. In the meantime, like his predecessor, he continued to entertain the Reeve and the local town Council with an annual lavish dinner in support of the retreat house. The special treat at these events was "Moose Milk," a mixture of one part rye whiskey and four parts liqueur, allowed to "mellow" for the previous week. Goodwill abounded.

Expanding the Property

Many retreatants would look across the ravine behind the retreat house and wonder: "Could we ever buy out that property? It would add so much more space for quiet reflection." Actually, an opportunity to buy the Ravine Hotel and Cottages had occurred earlier. Mr. and Mrs. Arthur Blair originally owned it. After Mr. Blair died in 1952, their daughter, Mrs. John O. Blair, living in Grosse Pointe, Michigan, was seriously thinking of selling. The hotel had a well-equipped kitchen, ten cottages, fourteen acres of land and 1,000 feet of lake frontage. In 1955, the diocesan chancellor, Msgr. Austin Roney, turned down their offer. He indicated "there were eight cities within the confines of the Diocese of London, each of which has to be provided with a retreat house in the future. It is impossible, therefore, to extend the facilities at Oxley until we have retreat houses in several other cities."[2] No deal. But what a vision for the retreat movement in the diocese!

Once again, an opportunity knocked on the door. Mrs. Blair was still willing to sell all of her property for $50,000.00. Bishop Carter made a visit to inspect the property. Fr. Gatfield, armed with his professional photographs of the property, gave the bishop a personal tour in his own car. The pressure was on. But this was not on the bishop's agenda. No deal. Eventually, Peter and Yolanda Cantarutti purchased the property. She was a very spiritual woman who took in abandoned children, raising them in a very Catholic atmosphere. Fr. Gatfield maintained a good friendship with them. But in his heart of hearts, he felt that a golden opportunity had been lost. To this day, Saturday night barbecues with country folk music from the resulting trailer camp continue to waft over the ravine invading the disciplined silence of the retreatants. Perhaps at another time....

Parking: a never-ending headache! Too many cars on the west side only of Victoria Street; too far to haul their luggage. Once again, Fr. Gatfield's landing instincts were activated. He and his Board looked east of their property to the other side of Victoria Street. Fr. Meloche had bought a piece of this property from the lake up to Prince Street, the laneway leading to the cottages, from a Mr. Pilon for $4500. He had planned to put up a building on it for the sisters and the volunteer women helping on the weekends. But it was insufficient for their needs. However, Fr. Gatfield managed to buy from Mr. De Melo another piece of this property which abutted the last house belonging to Mr. Cleghorn on the east side of Victoria Street. He was also hoping to reroute Victoria Street to form a bend around their newly acquired property which would

Looking east from the main gate (where the former Methodist church was located)

---

2   Letter of Sept. 19, 1955, from Rt. Rev. J. Austin Roney, D.P., Chancellor, responding to letter of S.C. Turner, Loan Agent in Detroit. London Archives.

provide a parking lot with no road in the middle. He even envisaged a new picket fence (with four sides, remember!) waiting to be painted by more eager seminarians.

One glitch: he needed to secure total ownership of a lane which descended from Victoria Street to the lake right in front of the retreat house area. Years ago this road had been used by a fisherman to deposit his fish there, to be picked up by cars and trucks driving down to the beach. Also, some local folk used this road to haul up sand from the beach.[3] Fr. Meloche had realized the legality that the road would have to be in non-use for seven years to claim total ownership.

Fr. Gatfield waded into the situation. He put double locks on the gates. The necessary time period elapsed, and they were able to extend their fence right to the lake. They bought the property on Victoria Street, but the plan to reroute Victoria Street never happened. The Board of Directors also put in the cruciform stone pieces on the beach to prevent erosion. Later in the 1990s, the government, using a huge barge and crane, put in a massive wall of large stones to further prevent Lake Erie from taking its toll on the bank.

The Saga of St. Joseph's House

In the midst of all these ecclesiastical shocks and property expansions, St. Joseph's House on the Western edge of the property faced a singular challenge all its own. Fr. Gatfield remembers that on one retreat, one rather portly retreat master, Fr. Dunstan, C.Ss.R., (called "The Banjo Priest"), was waxing eloquently seated on a chair on the porch of St. Joseph's House. It was a men's retreat with the men sitting facing the lake. As he droned on, his heavy set frame slowly began to disappear from view like a sunset, right in front of their eyes. The possibly sleepy eyes of the retreatants gaped with stark amazement. The floor of the porch was gradually descending to the ground! Fr. Dunstan needed instant rescuing. The cause? Termites! More fall-out from Vatican II?

Again, divine providence intervened. For some reason, the government in Ottawa was coming to the aid of Southwestern Ontario by a specific study of these devastating insects. For the next three years during the summer months, they sent learned scientists to study the termite situation. These men lived at the Ravine Cottages next door, spending their days on their hands and knees on the retreat grounds inserting small sticks into the earth. Fr. Gatfield says he even visited these fine folks in Ottawa and enjoyed sleeping in their termite-

---

3   It is interesting to note that, in the 1800s, just west of where the ravine drains into the lake, there was a landing place on the beach called "Oxford Wharf," part of the "Village of Oxford." See Diocesan archives.

Holy Family Retreat House, Oxley, Ont.

(Engraving on Retreat House letterhead)

ree homes! When their study was completed, a booklet was published about he termite infestation of Southwestern Ontario.[4] Fr. Gatfield says that Holy ʾamily Retreat House was the "Termite Capital of Southwestern Ontario!" This seems to be a far cry from its work as a spiritual home for people.

The building seemed in need of replacement. There was the large sum of noney left by Fr. Meloche to build a new chapel mentioned earlier. Fr. Loeʾach had given Fr. Gatfield some money which he had inherited from his famᴵy, but even this was not enough to build a new St. Joseph's Building. Could a ʾew building be constructed so close to the Lake and the ravine? He was ssured that it was feasible. Interestingly enough, Fr. Meloche had some granᴵiose dreams for a total remaking of *all* the buildings on the site. The plans for his remarkable centre, dated 1963, would have had a building with all the ʾooms facing the lake, complete with individual balconies. If it had come to ʾass, it would have been the envy of all of Southwestern Ontario. (See page 64 ʾor this contemplated design.)

By November, 1965, Fr. Gatfield was in building mode. He sent out a mis-ive to "the Representative of your parish of the building promotion of the ᵀoly Family Retreat League." At meetings at St. Clare's Auditorium in Wind-or, he cogently outlined why a whole new retreat house should be built: the ʾresent buildings arc of wooden construction, fifty years old, and built for a ʾummer residence only; bringing the present buildings up to date is cost-ʾrohibitive, ending up with only old buildings; great fire hazard for everyone ʾ"one match would destroy a building"); insurance rates are in proportion to he risk; deterioration within the walls, exemplified by the collapse of the ʾorch of St. Joseph's House; maintenance difficulties with the spread-out

4   See C.S. Kirby, *Termites in Ontario, with Particular Reference to the Toronto Region*, Can-ada, Department of Forestry and Rural Development, Forestry Branch, April, 1967; reprint from Information Report, 1963-1 dated April 1963, with references to "Oxley" on pp. 5(map) and 6.

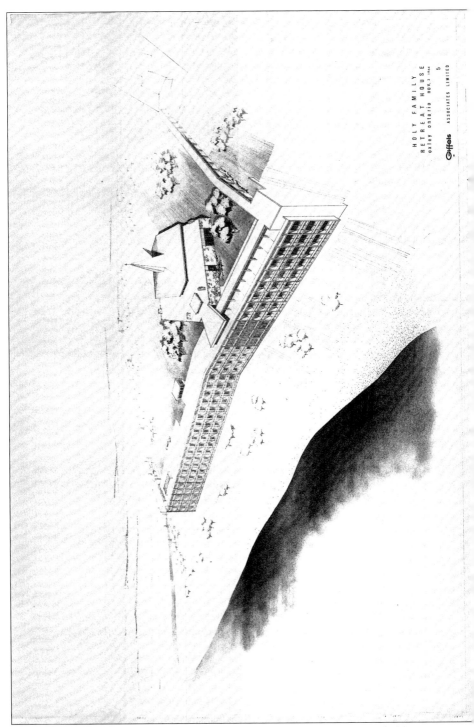

The "Dream" Retreat House of Frs. Meloche and Gatfield
(reprinted with permission)

aspect of the quaint but attractive five buildings, including heating and problems with inclement weather, especially when right on the lake moving from building to building; deterioration in spring time with St. Mary's building sinking toward the ravine; problems with the temporary, telephone pole supports for the St. Mary's building; too many labour hours spent walking from building to building. All this was not without countless headaches for Fr. Gatfield, whose engineering skills had now been pushed to the maximum.

With all these problems, his proposal went on to advocate the splendid new structure envisioned by Fr. Meloche, one whole new structure with all 96 rooms facing the lake, with balconies and individual washrooms, and with a brand new chapel attached behind the main building. The main building was to be built right onto the cliff! Fr. Doll opines: "A closeness to the water—the gripping of the infinity of space as you overlook the distant horizon...The chapel itself will be built on the main part of the property as an edifice of worship looming up to the sky and predominantly placed at the centre of the retreatants' life. When you walk in, you will see this structure—the core of our spirituality—the centre around which our life pivots...Cost to be $500,000 with $100,000 raised by retreatants. This does not include furnishings." Parishes would be asked to come up with $8,000, enough for one room. Bishop Carter mandated Fr. Gatfield "to get your teeth into the building program." Fr. Gatfield emphasized that this part of the diocese needs a "spiritual monument." His clincher: "The retreat house is the spiritual home of the lay person."

Fr. Gatfield recognized that he did not have the dynamism or the strength of Fr. Meloche. He did acknowledge that he had great strength with the combined efforts of the time, talents and guidance for God's work. "Operation—Moment of Truth" was launched. Sixty parishes reported on the feasibility of the proposal: 56.7%: "yes," some with qualifications; 26.7% "no," also with some qualifications; and 16.6% "undecided." By January 8, 1966, there was enough hesitation to force a re-evaluation of the whole project. There were heavy assessments for other purposes; involvement with the Christian Life Centre in Windsor, one of the side proposals, would confuse the purpose of the buildings; private baths gave an air of luxury; and finally, build on the bank? "It will fall into the lake!" Fr. Adrian Jansen would later repeatedly bellow!

In 1967, Canada celebrated her centennial as a country. The Holy Family Retreat League latched onto this event, and the new St. Joseph Building project became known as the Centennial Building Program. Plans were scaled down, the building on the cliff was abandoned, and a building was proposed for the same site as the decrepit "St. Joseph's Hostel," as some called it. It would contain 34 rooms (scaled down from 44). With all the funds they had raised so far, the projected cost of $240,000 including furnishings. With what they had already saved up, it would require a bank loan for $110,000 at 7¼%, to be repaid in five years. Enough impetus was present and approval was finally obtained from the Board and the Bishop.

In late 1968, Fr. Fred Doll, a strong supporter of the retreat house, suddenly produced a publication called *Oxley News*.[5] He intended it to be published monthly. Enjoy his colorful prose about the beginning of the new building:

"Now for the Real News — please sit down and hang on to your hat!

St. Joseph's House is gone, demolished, caput, finis. It is the place where you bought books, cigarettes, candy bars. Where you attended lectures, slept in cozy rooms rather than old and worn out as well as noisy at nights.

The banner of Fr. Doll's famous newsletter

"The Dumouchelle Bros. from McGregor, Ontario, tore down St. Joseph's hostel." [This cost $1,000, and took two-and-a-half weeks.]

"They keep the material, that is, what the busy termites did not eat. With St. Joseph's gone, it will be a hard winter for the termites. They will be cold and hungry. But we have not twinge of conscience; we fed

St. Joseph's House: "caput!"

them long enough with choice tidbits. May them immigrate to other properties in the country. Let them be ecumenical in their horizontal as well as vertical movements.

---

5   "*Oxley News*," Harrow, Ontario, Vol. 1, no. 2, Dec. 1968, from London Diocesan archives. This is the only number available. We have not corrected this text, leaving it as it is in the original publication.

"Are you still sitting down? Or perhaps you are picking yourself up off the floor. Well in either case, remain where you are as you here is earth shattering news. At this very moment, the New St. Joseph Building is going up. The Kehl Construction Co. of Harrow, Ontario, has agreed to erect the building. The total furnished cost will be $240,000. Our Architect is Mr. Robert Langlois of Sheppard, Mason, Brand and Langlois. The figure provides new beds (double), fixed headboards, lamps, comfortable chair

St. Joseph Building risen from the debris!

(hurrah), table, drapes, and wall to wall carpeting for each retreatant's rooms, Fr. Gatfield's room, Fr. Beuglet's rooms, the lounge and entrance foyer."

The rest of this issue describes efforts to raise money to pay off the loan. The weekly Bingo at the Teutonia Club in Windsor would donate one week's earnings per month, approximately $1,000, for the retreat house. Volunteers were requested to help out. Parishes would be asked to raise $8,000 each. Individuals were invited to join the "Friends of the Retreat League" for $1.00. Their names would be inscribed in a "Friendship Book." The issue concluded with pictures featuring the 20th Anniver-

Dinner at the Prince Edward Hotel, Windsor

sary celebration of the retreat house on September. 15, 1968, with an outdoor Mass with Frs. Meloche, Gatfield and Beuglet concelebrating. The Centennial Building Program would soon be completed.

The Waning of his Retreat Energy

By 1968, Frs. Gatfield and Beuglet were into new ways of presenting retreats. Fr. Gatfield praised Fr. Beuglet, his associate director, for his specific efforts to provide a highly successful youth program, being "by far the finest with his adept use of visual aids such as films, tape recorders, records, and his

own highly talented approach."[6] In February, they also provided a one-week retreat called "Movement for a Better World Retreat." Fr. Riccardo Lombardi, S.J., had recently founded this format in Rocca di Papa near Rome. It was repeated the following year. These retreats involved a team of two or three

Fr. Gatfield; priest/tour guide (name not known); the author (back row); and Fr. Meloche (seated)

leaders, namely a priest, sister or brother, and a laywoman. The format aimed at bringing together all the vocations in the church to provide a spiritual renewal. Much personal sharing fleshed out the approach. It was a new variation on the silent or "closed" retreat.

However, all this was not without countless headaches for Fr. Gatfield. To add to his troubles, he started losing some of his treasured Secular Institute women from Spain, who were a God-send. Using their original charism of retreat ministry, they had provided a wonderful spiritual home for himself and the retreatants. But with his acute perception, Bishop Carter started to take note of the remarkable talents of these women. So, he began to "raid" the retreat house. Beth Tellaeche (along with Angela Aisa, who was not at the retreat house then) ended up working for him at the chancery office in London. Then, Araceli Echebarria was seconded to became his housekeeper. Replacing them proved to be a further drain on Fr. Gatfield.

With all this on his mind after completing almost five years as director of the retreat house, Fr. Gatfield realized that he needed to get away for a change. His own energies needed a renewal. In 1969, he headed up to Quebec to stay with some friends at a place called Notre Dame de la Mercie. He was at total peace of mind and this was just what the doctor ordered. His next assignment

6   *Ibid.*, p. 7.

took him to St. Anthony's parish in Harrow, Ontario, right next to his beloved retreat house. He remained there, loved by all, for seventeen years. Bringing his life to full circle, he is now retired in the peaceful family home he so fondly loves, right on the Detroit River.

As he muses on all of his connections to the retreat house, Fr. Gatfield overflows with grateful and peaceful emotion.[7] He strongly attributes the beginning and fostering of his priestly vocation to Fr. Meloche. He has no doubt that the close relationship to the Retreat Movement in the diocese helped him to have an outlook that is truly Catholic: inclusive, open to learn about the faith from every source sent along by God, able to trust and employ the gifts of lay people, and depending on God and the sacraments, especially the Eucharist, for his daily spiritual sustenance. At his home, he continues to be filled with wonder and awe at everything from a hummingbird to a large freighter silently floating by his large bay window.

Perhaps one of his favorite lines from scripture provides the ultimate encomium to his dedication to the retreat movement: "God has done marvelous things in me." (*Luke* 1:49)

Wendy Wright (left), Fr. Ted, Kathy Peters, and Nita Kosokowsky

7   It is worth noting that all of Fr. Gatfield's numerous photos (including the negatives), plus his wonderful photos of many of the alumni reunions of St. Peter's Seminary in London, are housed at the Marsh Foundation in Amherstburg, Ontario.

chapter 5

Fr. Charlie Beuglet
"Enthusiastic Youth Retreat Director"

Assistant Director from 1967-1969

By 1967, the retreat load had increased so significantly that Fr. Gatfield needed a priest-assistant. Not only that, but further pressures prevailed: the termites had won! The old St. Joseph's Building was about to be torn down and construction would begin on a new building. Retreats were still being held, but on a smaller scale in St. Mary's Building and the Nazareth House. Bishop Carter, the ordinary of the London diocese since 1964, had just that person on deck.

Enter Fr. Charlie Beuglet. Born in 1936 in Tecumseh, Ontario, he received his education in Tecumseh, Windsor, Ottawa, and St. Peter's Seminary. Bishop Nelligan ordained him in the seminary chapel on December 23, 1961. His pastoral work included Our Lady of Sorrows in Aylmer, Immaculate Conception, Windsor and St Andrew's, London. In 1967, Bishop Carter made him Assistant Director of the retreat house, to provide the needed support for Fr. Gatfield. He was assigned to a room in the old St. Joseph's Building.

l. to r.: Fr. Meloche, Fr. Gatfield and Fr. Beuglet celebrate an outdoor Mass at the 20th anniversary

He was enthusiastic, focused, dedicated and gregarious — great charac-

Fr. Beuglet celebrates the Eucharist with his beloved young people

teristics to have in the turbulent nineteen-sixties. He spoke with direct honesty. When given a job, he did it with vim, vitality and vigour. Fr. Ted put him in charge of the numerous young people's retreats being held at Oxley. Indeed, if there was no adult retreat on the weekend, they usually filled the weekend with a youth retreat, bringing in mostly high school seniors.

Deep thoughts for retreatants

Fr. Beuglet was a very successful youth retreat master. In his first six months at the retreat house, they even hired outside retreat masters to conduct these retreats. By about September, 1968, he was put in charge of all the youth retreats. It must be remembered that almost 100% of the youth retreats at that time were comprised of students from Detroit. The Holy Family Retreat House had a terrific reputation among the parochial and private schools in the Archdiocese of Detroit. Fr. Beuglet was so popular with the young Americans that, when he left the retreat house in 1969, he was invited to conduct some of his scheduled retreats in Detroit. He happily agreed.

Fr. Gatfield praised all of his associate's skills in glowing terms in the only extant issue that we can find of *Oxley News* in 1968. He chastised Fr. Doll, the editor of this tiny broadsheet, for extolling himself and ignoring Fr. Beuglet: "What he failed to do was point out the reason for our success, in the presence of Father Beuglet, associate Director, and Director of our highly successful youth program. It is by far the finest with his adept use of visual aids such as films, tape recorders, records, and his own highly talented approach."[1]

Praise for All the Staff

It is noteworthy to mention some other individuals whom Fr. Gatfield lavishly praised in his article when Fr. Beuglet was working at the retreat house. He specifically mentions the members of the Lay Institute, namely Julia (Zalbidea), "…about whom the office pivots, with her genial way of prodding us to see our financial condition, and keeping us aware of our recruiting. She cannot be matched for her splendid public relations with you all via telephone, personal contacts and letters. She had a wonderful trip home to Spain this summer, and is back with a freshness and the fullness of Spanish liveliness."[2] He goes on to extol the additional services of Nora (Aragones), who did not return with Julia, and Araceli (Echevarria), who still served from 600 to 800 meals a week. Not to be

St. Francis of Assisi, corner of St. Joseph Building

---

1   "From the Desk of the Director Rev. Edward P. Gatfield," *Oxley News*, Vol. 1, no. 2 (December, 1968), 7. I have added the full names, in brackets, with the help of Ruth Beitia.

2   *Ibid.*

left out was Ruth (Beitia), whom he called "the spirit of our home, and with her never tiring work to keep our place organized. She constantly is performing miracles to keep everything in order since we have been handling two retreats a week. She is aided by our ever-loving Theresa (Egervari) to whom the retreat house is so grateful. Along with Theresa we are helped now by Joanna (Franco) and Mrs. (Teresa) Schwager and Maria (Damaso)."[3]

He goes on to thank Christine Serrano for her work in the office during Julia's absence, especially her artistic talents around the retreat house. Ted Boutette is praised for his seventeen years as maintenance engineer, along with his wife Beatrice and their family, Mr. Anton Frank, for being the "sage" on premise, Jo-anne Johnson and her friends, and, Wilma Gelinas who helped every weekend. The retreat house was humming right along at high speed.

More on the Saga of St. Joseph's Building

As we saw earlier, the design for the new St. Joseph's Building had created more room for the increasing number of retreatants who were expected at Oxley. The "Ravine Room" was in the works, but Fr. Beuglet felt strongly that a conference room in its basement would also be necessary. To his credit, his suggestion prevailed over the strong resistance of some of the Board. It was a felicitous suggestion. The new building was still located precariously close to the edge of the bank on the lake. Indeed, this room along with the Ravine Room upstairs would also help to keep the whole building stabilized, through a "cantilever balance" effect (to quote Fr. Jansen). Who would have thought?

When the wrecking ball did hit St. Joseph's House, Fr. Ted and Fr. Charlie moved to Cana House on (then) Highway 18A. The Boutettes were living in a big house three doors over. The new building was soon completed and retreats carried on. When Fr. Gatfield took a sick leave in 1969, Fr. Beuglet became the Interim Director with the added responsibility to oversee construction of the new St. Joseph Building.

However, tensions developed between Fr. Beuglet and some of the Secular Institute women on staff. He had hoped to bring in Sr. Maureen Fay, a Dominican sister from Adrian, Michigan, to help him give the retreats. Difficulties with this flared up, and two of the Secular Institute women, Ruth and Julia, moved to Windsor, while the rest remained at Oxley. Sr. Maureen did come and help Fr. Beuglet as his assistant for three or four months, but then departed. The tensions led to Bishop Carter replacing Fr. Beuglet with Fr. Adrian Jansen in December of 1969. Fr. Beuglet had done his best to carry on the retreat house tradition at Oxley.

Fr. Adrian Jansen, the next retreat house director, invited the Secular

_____

3   *Ibid.*

Institute women to return and two of them did. Along with Fr. Jansen, they were one of the threads of continuity for Holy Family Retreat House for many more years.

Fr. Beuglet went on to do a Master's degree in communications from New York University in New York. In 1974, he obtained his law degree from McGill University in Montreal. After graduating from McGill, he became Executive Assistant to Warren Allmand, Solicitor General of Canada, and Human Resource Vice-President for a pharmaceutical company in Montreal. He then went on to practice law in Southern California until recently. He now owns a men's sober living house in Costa Mecca, California, where fourteen men live in early sobriety. After being freed from his priestly commitment to celibacy, he married Catherine Cole, M.D., who died in 1987. They had a son who was seven years old at the time of her death. He raised him alone.

Fr. Beuglet's efforts at the retreat house provided much spiritual hope and comfort to people coming to Oxley for a religious renewal. His own personal enthusiasm, eager spirit and struggles with the changes of Vatican II, undoubtedly resonated with the retreatants, both young and old, who probably experienced many similar ups and downs in those tumultuous times. It is noteworthy that his presence at the retreat house was somewhat foreseen by the beautiful concrete statue of the Holy Family donated by his parents, Dr. and Mrs. Ernest Beuglet, in 1948.

Fr. Beuglet's legacy will continue to be his fresh energizing of the youth retreats at that time, and his insistence on the basement conference room at St. Joseph's Building. This turned out to be a natural bridge for the retreat activities of his dynamic successor, Fr. Adrian Jansen.

Affirmations

Sat. Oct 21/06

Dear Jesus,

Thank you for allowing for me to be on this beautiful Charismatic Retreat here at Oxley. You are surely with me and you are healing all my hurts & pains throughout my life. This place is so beautiful, the rooms, the meals, the grounds it's breath-taking. I can really feel the sense of peace here.

God Bless everyone.

M.D.P.

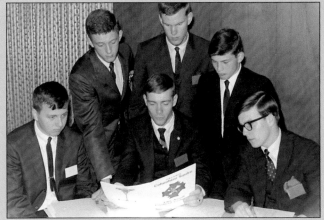

chapter 6

Fr. Adrian Jansen
"Something Beautiful for God"

Director from 1970–1988

I first met him in 1955 when he was chaplain at Corpus Christi High School (now F.J. Brennan) in Windsor, Ontario. He was full of energy, loved all of us students, and had an enormous love of culture of every kind. His favorite opera: *La Bohème*; his favorite composer: Mozart. Most of all, he was a joyful priest who loved to talk about the Catholic faith. He seemed to have read everything, but especially the Fathers of the Church and the great classics of literature. He would cite these with great *éclat* from the current reading of *The Liturgy of the Hours*. He loved to remind us that philosophy is the *ancilla*, or handmaid, of theology. They go together. He would frequently sum up our Catholicity with a bellowing proclamation: "**Sacraments, sacraments, sacraments!**" Emphatic, decisive, prayerful, current, a critical thinker, truly magisterial—like his photo, complete with midnight black cape and biretta—this is Fr. Adrian Jansen. Someone worth knowing—and respecting!

The seminarian Adrian as a chef

Born on July 23, 1919, in Rotterdam, Holland, he grew up in Holy Name of Mary parish ("Our Lady of Prompt Succor" in those days) under the astute tutelage of Msgr. (Pippi) Rooney. Not surprisingly, he was one of the priestly grads of the famous "Pippi Rooney Priestly Vocation School," one of the countless vocations to the priesthood that blossomed under his record fifty-year pastorate of the parish. He entered the seminary, but left after only one year to return to the military, where he had served briefly before entering the seminary. He served in World War II, specifically on the hospital ship *Laetitia*, in both the Atlantic and the Pacific Ocean;

after the war, it was back to the seminary. It must be noted that he was one of the seminarians who had worked at the retreat house during the summertime. He had fallen under the influence of the Fr. Meloche "summer seminary training grounds." He remembers that he even found the chapel bell abandoned in the ravine just in time to install it for the grand opening in 1948. It was used to call everyone for meals. He was ordained in 1952 in a class with two later episcopal members, Bishops James Mahoney of Saskatoon and Eugène LaRocque of Windsor.

In spite of ongoing health issues, Fr. Jansen has had a rich life as a priest. He served St. Joseph parish in Windsor for two years, then ministered at Hôtel Dieu Hospital in Windsor as chaplain for four years. For eight years, he was chaplain at Corpus Christi High School. More parish work ensued: one year as pastor of St. Joseph parish in Sarnia, four years at Our Lady of Mount Carmel parish in Mount Carmel, Ontario, and then eleven months at St. Benedict parish in Sarnia. But then, the "retreat movement influence," dormant in him since seminary days, flared up in his priestly heart. From 1970–1988, he mightily orchestrated retreat life at Oxley.

He was no stranger to retreats, as he had preached all kinds of retreats, prayer days and missions in his pastoral life. A born teacher, he loved to craft presentations rich in biblical and cultural imagery, along with wonderfully insightful commentaries on the latest movements and challenges to the faith. He also thrived on being a good confessor and spiritual director. He moved smoothly in education circles, but not without an occasional outburst of emotion when defending the faith or when someone's rights demanded it. He made a perfect fit to follow the brief stint of Fr. Beuglet at the retreat house.

He is a wonderful purveyor of many "oral traditions" about the retreat house. As I indicated in my introduction, our spiritual directors' late evening *soirées* with him during our own annual directed retreats with the seminarians provided rich fodder for our hungry ears (and thirsty mouths!). Fr. Jack O'Flaherty was especially adroit in lobbing loaded questions to him that elicited responses, which, like his mentor Fr. Meloche, always enjoyed a high degree of infallibility. His love of God, our Catholic faith and the Church has remained rock solid. He is a true Catholic apologist.

Retreat House Developments

Fr. Jansen remembers the wonderful cooks he had in the kitchen, including Theresa Egervari, Teresa Schwager, Joanna Franco, Maria Damaso and the famous "Alex" of early days. When he first began, his staff included Ted Boutette as groundskeeper and Maria Demarco in the office. He also praised Alice Surneels who did a "terrific job" as his bookkeeper and secretary. He continued to enjoy the presence of the Secular Institute women, who returned after their brief departure under the previous administration. Ruth Beitia, I.S.M., remained with him the longest. She took on iconic status with her constant Spanish smile and warm hospitality to everyone. In later years, Al Cardinal came on board to assist with various aspects of managing the retreat house. In addition, a number of teenage and adult volunteers came to help every weekend. Among them, Cathy Cloutier deserves special mention for

A happy Fr. Jansen with Ruth Beitia, I.S.M.

the tremendous assistance she provided for many years.

Various improvements emerged in the chapel. Fr. Jansen introduced a wrought-iron ambo and candlesticks, along with a table for the tabernacle. Other hand-carved artwork added new inspiration. He loves to tell how the appointments in the chapel (the artwork, the altarpiece, the statues of Mary washing a dish and Joseph holding a hammer, the Stations of the Cross and the Infant of Prague) were all hand-carved by the same person, Mr. J. Rylko. They cost $5,066. However, he loves to tell the story of correcting an important detail about the beautiful wooden frieze of the crucifixion behind the altar:

"He was a refugee from Hungary and lived in Delhi. I was there when all the stuff was brought in. I was a visitor then, one year ordained and

Mr. Rylko's frieze behind the altar in the chapel

going to visit him in Delhi where we had a great conversation about the altarpiece. When I saw the drawings — full-size drawings sketched out on the table — they were asking Fr. Meloche for his approval. I kept looking at it and said 'no', there is something wrong here, something wrong, and finally I figured it out. They had the good thief at the right hand of the picture of the artwork. They had replaced the good thief at Jesus' left hand and scripture plainly said that the good thief was on Jesus' right hand. So it had to be inverted. The artist started to laugh and Fr. Meloche said he hadn't noticed. Since I spent all those years at the retreat house, it would have killed me to see that artwork with the good thief on the wrong side of our Lord which would have driven me to distraction."[1]

Clearly, Fr. Jansen knew his scriptures *and* prayed them with Ignatian detail!

The waves of Lake Erie relentlessly ravaged the shoreline and the bluff

Endless views from the bank of the lake

above it. 1976 was an especially stormy year, costing the retreat house some 10 meters (30 feet) of lake frontage due to erosion. One day, Fr. Jansen was standing with a hydraulic engineer near the bluff to determine the cliff's stability. "Oh Father, there's nothing to worry about. This will be here long after we are gone," assured the engineer. An hour later, the cliff edge where Fr. Jansen had been standing, was washed into the lake. "It makes you wonder!" mused Fr. Jansen, possibly thinking about the location of St. Joseph's Building.

When Fr. Jansen became director of the retreat house, the new St. Joseph's

---

1   See Adrian Jansen, "St. Peter's Seminary and Holy Family Retreat House: Another Vital Connection," *The Alumni Bulletin — 1996–1997*, no. 57 (December, 1997), pp. 34–36.

House still had to be paid off, a sum of some $50,000. He applied himself to the task by preaching missions, giving talks, and doing all kinds of retreat activities at the retreat house. With help from the diocese, he managed to clear off the whole debt.

Various Groups of Retreatants

I mentioned that the seminarians began to have their annual directed retreat at Oxley in 1974. This was only one of the groups making retreats at this time. Other retreats included weekend retreats for men, women, and various parishes. The groups also included students preparing to be confirmed (usually day sessions), Alcoholics Anonymous (including one all-gay group), as well as Protestant groups that included Lutherans, Anglicans and members of the United Church. Students also came from Bishop Gallagher High School in Detroit for various kinds of prayer days and retreats. Fr. Jansen's unique ability to illustrate the demands of our Catholic faith used all kinds of audio-visual materials, scriptural and literary allusions along with catchy human life stories. This form of teaching became especially memorable in dealing with the demands of the virtue of premarital chastity. *Everyone* seems to remember his famous line: "When you come to your wedding day, be able to say "I do" not "I didn't." Titters always rustled among the young folk gathered at his feet.

Happy workers and volunteers

Fr. Jansen continued to promote weekend retreats for surrounding parishes. Like his predecessor, Fr. Meloche, he would make weekend forays into the parishes, proclaim the Good News at Mass, and give a

Fr. Jansen and his beloved young folk

strong pitch for the necessity of a silent retreat in order to grow in one's spiritual life. Some of the local pastors were indomitable supporters of the retreat house. Fr. Fred Doll in Kingsville frequently recruited enough of his own parishioners to fill a whole weekend. In the 1980s, the cost was $50 for a weekend, or $70 if from outside the diocese. With some 6,000 retreatants annually, the retreat house still ran an annual deficit of $25,000 to $30,000, with the tab fortunately picked up by the diocese, and hence the higher fee for those outside the diocese.

At one point, the board wanted Fr. Jansen to drop retreats for young people, since the charge of a mere $4 per person per day was deemed inadequate. Bishop Carter himself vetoed this, showing his constant support of Fr. Jansen and the retreat house. Thus, he could continue to affirm these young people with his signature acclaim: "You're beautiful! You're good! Nobody tells them these things." They kept coming and they kept quoting him for the rest of their lives.

A Legendary Legacy

Fr. Paul Crunican, a deceased classmate of Fr. Jansen, once penned a beautiful tribute to him: "Some people see the darker side of life; others find beauty

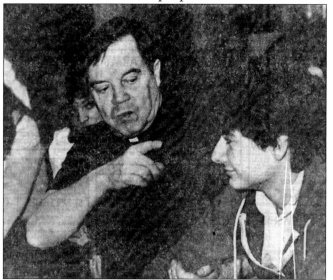

"You can do it!"

in unexpected places. …His characteristic phrase is 'That's beautiful!' At Holy Family Retreat House he made innumerable long-time friends. He is noted for his enthusiasm in giving retreat days for young people." Bishop Emmett Carter once underlined this: Fr. Jansen "tries to wake up what kids don't have from grade school and he succeeds." His methodology for instructing young people was to start with the five senses, stimulate them with all the natural wonders around the retreat house and in their lives, and allow their spirituality to catch up.

One well-known local reporter did a two-page feature on Fr. Jansen in 1983. He pointed out that Fr. Jansen is like a politician in that he never forgets a face, but he is *unlike* one in that he actually *doesn't* forget, while politicians only pretend to have such power of recall. He goes on to cite one of the staff members about Fr. Jansen's approach to the faith. With valid insight, he stated: "He sounds trad-itional, but really isn't …dealing on a one-to-one basis, he's the most open-minded priest ever…and he really does listen."[2]

Rob Van Nie in an article in *The Windsor Star* quotes Fr. Jansen about the aim of a retreat: "to help people find God in ordinary things." This percep-tion is based on a state-ment by the painter Andrew Wyeth: Fr. Jansen "tries to invoke a sensation of the infi-nite in the common-place." He continues to explain how we need silence, which today is becoming a real luxury. The retreats

Christ the King Chapel: where God meets his people

at Oxley have always promoted a high degree of silence, one of the hallmarks of these much-cherished spiritual renewals.

On April 19, 2010, I interviewed Fr. Jansen yet again on what perspectives are necessary for the retreat house in the 21st century. He insisted that retreatants need help to deepen their faith. They need more doctrine, espe-cially young people. When asked to identify the highlight of his whole priest-hood (at the "tender" age of 90), he simply said: "To have celebrated one Mass." I think we can epitomize him by borrowing Malcolm Muggeridge's famous encomium about Mother Teresa: "Something beautiful for God." The two have a lot in common.

---

2   Marty Gervais, "He'll put you in touch with yourself," *The Windsor Star*, Jan. 22, 1983, p. D10.

chapter 7

Fr. Dan Rocheleau
"An Unfulfilled Dream"

Director from 1988–1990

Fr. Dan had a dream: to be at Holy Family Retreat House some day. He was a priest from Holy Name of Mary parish in Windsor, Ontario. Ordained in 1975, he has served in many parishes, including St. Andrew the Apostle, London; St. Benedict, Sarnia; St. John the Divine, London; Our Lady of Mercy, Sarnia; and, St. Patrick, London. He has also served as the Chaplain of Mount St. Joseph, London and the Priest Chaplain for the London Health Sciences Centre and St. Joseph's Health Care, London.

He has always had a penchant for spirituality. It is not surprising that he was delighted that Bishop Sherlock asked him to undertake graduate studies in spirituality with the plan to replace Fr. Jansen when he would retire, challenging as that might have seemed. He would be the new director. So, in the summer of 1986, Fr. Dan was accepted at St. John's University in Minnesota in their Master's program in Theology. In the spring of 1988, he was granted the degree of Master of Arts in Theology with a concentration in Spirituality and Spiritual Direction. He found all this a blessed experience, yet not without new challenges on many

Anniversary celebration card

levels. Studying spirituality rarely leaves one's soul untouched. As it happened, Fr. Jansen actually did surrender to retirement that same summer and Fr. Dan tried to fill his shoes as director, an indomitable task.

His Plan

Fr. Dan quickly decided not to eliminate any of the programs that had been in place for many years. He did, however, intend to broaden the mandate of the retreat house in order to address more needs of the adult faith community of

the diocese. He had high hopes that Oxley would truly become a unique centre of spirituality—the "spiritual heart" of the diocese. This was his fresh vision

for "the seminary of
the laity" envisioned
by Bishop Kidd on
opening day.

Early in the fall of
1989, Sr. Kathleen
Lichti, C.S.J., and
Sr. Emma Bezaire,
S.N.J.M., were work-
ing out of Holy
Redeemer College as
retreat leaders and
spiritual directors.
They joined Fr. Dan as
volunteer staff, helping him with new programming and providing invaluable
support. Also at this time, Fr. Dan formed a new Board of Directors with rep-
resentatives from each Deanery of the diocese. The mandate of the new Board
was to oversee all operational aspects of the retreat house.

But very soon, his dream faltered; lack of money became the primary
focus. Fr. Jansen had always found it hard to make ends meet. Retreat houses,

Sr. Kateri Ghesquiere, C.S.J.,
Fr. Dan, Sr. Claire Marie
Pageau, C.S.J.

almost by definition, are not self-supporting.
For Fr. Dan, the situation became acute. Al
Cardinal had been the Business Manager
before his arrival on the scene. With no funds
available, the diocese steadfastly refused the
capital required to maintain the status quo,
but also to make long overdue changes to the
physical plant. In January of 1990, Bishop
Sherlock informed Fr. Dan that the retreat
house would be closed as of March, 1990.
Staff were out of a job. No other reasons were given. Fr. Dan was devastated.
On leaving the retreat house, he took an eight-month leave of absence before
being appointed as Pastor of Our Lady of Mercy parish in Sarnia. He served
in two parishes for the next thirteen years before assuming hospital chap-
laincy work in London. In spite of numerous health issues, he soldiers on
faithfully in this priestly ministry.

Fr. Dan fleshed out further details about his tenure at the retreat house.
He recalls that when Ruth Beitia retired, after serving the retreat house so

faithfully with Fr. Jansen as housekeeper and receptionist, Jerry and Mary Ann Tracey along with their teenage children moved into her house on the property. Mary Ann became the head housekeeper and staff supervisor while her husband continued teaching at Mercy College in Michigan. They had been longtime parishioners in Kingsville, even selling their own home to commit themselves to ministry at the retreat house. When the retreat house closed, they were left without a home and decided to  move their family to Michigan. It was a painful departure.

A few months after the closure, the diocese hired Sr. Shirley McAuley, O.S.U. and Sr. Rose Marie Rau, O.S.U. to operate the retreat house. Fr. Dan's personal note on this move breathes deep faith: "Like manna in the desert, the money to operate the facility miraculously appeared!" How this happened will lead us into our next chapter.

Fr. Dan's priesthood has been full of many kinds of suffering. His constant spiritual yearnings seemed like the right mix to try to follow the giant leadership at the retreat house under Fr. Jansen. But a number of financial constraints weighed down the diocese, and the overall retreat movement was beginning to wane. This proved to be too much for the somewhat quiet and sensitive temperament of Fr. Dan. It would take another quite different personality to resurrect the temporarily defunct Holy Family Retreat House. It is to Fr. Dan's credit that he took stock of himself and returned to an active priestly ministry with a special concern for the sick and for seniors. Like Moses, someone else would fulfill his unfulfilled dream. And a fresh diocesan plan in the twenty-first century would yet again envision Holy Family Retreat House as the "Spiritual Heart" of the diocese. The saga continues to unfold.

Fr. Dan with friends Ted Lynch and Sue Tremblay

Sad to say, Fr. Rocheleau died peacefully on November 27, 2010.

chapter 8

Sr. Shirley McAuley, OSU
"Creative Refurbisher"

Director from 1990–1994

The retreat house needed a facelift. Fr. Jansen had done his best with the limited funds he could muster. Fr. Rocheleau's difficulties prevented him from making any real forward strides, either by way of fresh programs or by refurbishing facilities and the grounds. Things looked seedy and the outlook was bleak. Had it served its purpose in the diocese?

Enter Sr. Shirley McAuley, a wonderful "mover and shaker" in the Ursuline community.[1] Born in Tecumseh, Ontario, she had entered the Ursuline Sisters in Chatham, Ontario, and spent her vocation teaching in both elementary and high schools. She even returned to her home town to teach at St. Anne High School. She also spent time as the director of the John XXIII Adult Education Centre in Windsor. Her leadership skills were further honed with eight years on the community's general leadership. Previously, she was the local superior of the Mother House Community in Chatham. Not surprisingly, these credentials made her a solid choice for Bishop Sherlock to invite her to do what she could to refurbish the retreat house. He gave her two years.

She admits that she had never tried something without succeeding. This is an introduction to her powerful personality: friendly, warm, compassionate, influential, demanding, creative, and loaded with energy. She has an amazing ability to tap into people's personal talents and gifts, as well as their generosity to help a charitable cause. Years of teaching in the Essex County area had endeared her to countless students and others in the community. She kept in touch with many of them, providing a solid base for requesting help for her various initiatives at the retreat house. She was the first woman director of Holy Family Retreat House. The "Seminary for the Laity" took on a fresh perspective.

---

1   Much of this chapter is based on interviews with the Ursuline Sisters, especially Sr. Shirley McAuley, Sr. Loretta Mitchell and Sr. Rose Marie Rau.

Refurbishing Holy Family Retreat House

The retreat house seemed dormant when she and Sr. Marguerite Lebert, another Ursuline, walked under the "Holy Ground" arch on April 1, 1990. Their first instincts were that it needed a "new broom." Finances were at a low ebb. Morale was low. Parts of the family house were literally falling down inside. They immediately realized that the family occupying the house must leave to begin the improvements. Sr. Rose Marie Rau would certainly remain to keep some kind of continuity. She served with her joyful spirit from 1989–2006. She was a "natural" to continue as secretary, do the bookkeeping, give retreats and spiritual direction, and engage in the ministry of hospitality. Sr. Margarete Lebert would take charge of housekeeping and attend to those making private retreats. Sr. Dorothy Dean, a Holy Name Sister, was also invited to come out and help part time to welcome the groups coming for a retreat. These last two sisters would stay until 1992.

Sr. Rosie in high gear!

The sisters had landed on the site like a team of spring cleaners. The "new broom" swept fast and clean. One of their first jobs was to spiff up the family house. It did not take them long to repaint rooms, fix dangling light fixtures, and make the house more habitable. It now became the residence for Sr. Rosie, Sr. Marguerite and Sr. Dorothy. Sr. Shirley chose to live in the director's suite on the main floor of St. Joseph Building.

Their renovating zeal intensified. Walking around the grounds, they found eleven holes that needed filling. Money was found, help requested and the job was done. The dining room had to be painted. The three of them charged into the work. Done! Claire and Ken Turner came in from Port Dover to help with painting and the annual budget. Ken was also the chair of the board for several years. The basement of the chapel was full of "stuff." Removed! Stairs needed rebuilding. Again, with help, done! The individual bedrooms for the retreatants all needed a complete facelift. With her seemingly endless list of "contacts," Sister Shirley invited individuals and married couples to finance the complete redecoration of one of the rooms according to their individual tastes. However, they still had to remember that it was a retreat house and not a high-class hotel. Linens, bedspreads, pillowcases and prayerful pictures, all with good taste, variety, relaxing, sometimes with a welcoming feminine touch…everything transformed each room. All these wonderful donors simply requested that each person using

Each room was uniquely and tastefully done.

the room would offer up a small prayer for them while they were on retreat. Their names were engraved on plaques on the door. It worked. Their repayment was one free weekend at Oxley. They would ask to use the room they had decorated when they returned for a retreat. The end result: all rooms were decorated at almost no charge!

The retreat house needed a chaplain. Fr. Robert Howell, C.S.B., was available and joined the team in August of 1990, remaining until March, 1991. To replace him, along came Fr. Alan Dufraimont in November of 1991, who had just finished a sabbatical. He readily accepted the position offered by the bishop. He stayed until June of 1992 to be followed by Fr. Dermot Fitzpatrick, C.Ss.R., who stayed for one year. Then, in August of 1993, Fr. Des Scanlon, C.Ss.R., came on board, having just retired from his latest job with the school board. God was providing once again with these wonderful priestly ministers.

Within the first month of their arrival, Sr. Rose Marie and Sr. Shirley headed off to one of the local town meetings in the nearby town of Harrow. They introduced themselves to the town council, announced that the retreat house was under new management, and generously offered them "anything we can do for you." Shortly after that, a huge gas explosion rocked downtown Harrow. Remembering their offer, the town officials sent the residents of a nursing home to the retreat house for a temporary stay. She thinks this gesture helped them when they needed a tax exemption from the government. This story is coming up a bit later.

Sr. Shirley's creative spirit envisaged countless ideas requiring carpentry work. She invited Louis Gouin of Tecumseh, Ontario, and the members of the St. Vincent de Paul Society to help finance these ventures. Now, enter Gaetan "Gates" Therrien, retired "Master Carpenter," who could rival the builders of Noah's ark with his craftsmanship. He was just what her creative genius needed. She strongly felt that prayer can be aided by suitable settings. To help this aim, she dreamed of a small addition on the second floor of the west end of St. Joseph Building. It would provide a beautiful location to view the lake, hear the waves and the birds, or watch the marvels of a storm brewing in the southwestern sky over the lake, all the while praising the Creator. She had Gates build this lofty lookout, designated "The Oasis." She also had him construct a retractable table there that could be used for early morning Masses after praying *The Liturgy of the Hours*. The altar has not survived but the room with its chairs for meditation persists to this day.

Her creative spirit and Gates' carpentry wizardry knew no bounds. The

The Eagle's Nest

The Cozy Cabin

stairs leading down to the lake were rebuilt, along with a small room for prayer half-way down. It was called "The Eagle's Nest." Behind St. Joseph's House, he tore down the small icehouse that was there and built a small cabin on the foundation. To refresh weary retreatants, enough plumbing was present to allow for installation of a Jacuzzi. "The Hiding Place" was born. A dilapidated shed at the far northern end of the property was completely renovated, thereby providing a cozy cabin with complete facilities for a hermit-like repose for a couple. The biggest disturbance would be the occasional barking of Charlie, the dog belonging to the neighbours living behind the cabin. It has now morphed into a storage place for lawn mowers and other equipment.

Her perhaps most outlandish dream made Gates wince, but he did it. Just outside Emmanuel House stands a large, forked ash tree with amazing "tree-house potential." Sure enough, Gates was able to construct a kind of tree-house which every young teenager would envy. "Zacck's Place" appeared on high. Climbing up to it demanded some agility, but once there, meditating on the story of Zaccheus (*Luke* 19:1–10) could possibly bring Ignatian contemplation to new heights, or, so she hoped! However, raccoons invaded it, school children used it as a playhouse, insurance problems emerged, and the ladder disappeared. Zacck's Place is just that: only a place, still towering above and perhaps haunted by its previous contemplatives.

Her refurbishing eyes zeroed in again on the rooms and the grounds. But where were those hidden donors needed to enhance them? Who could generously provide knick-knacks for the various rooms? A jeweller, of course! Sandra Parent, her cousin,

Zacck's Place

of Birk's Jewellers in Toronto, got a phone call. Some out-of-date items were available. Done! Who has a green-thumb to revitalize the grounds? Vicki and Dennis Ullyett of Windsor to the rescue! Fresh plants and flowers suddenly seemed to bloom everywhere. Year after year they ensured that the flora did not languish. She also called a man named "Kelly" who had donated many trees from the municipality for the retreat house. He came every year to trim them. Nazareth House needed new cupboards. Mr. Larivière from Windsor did the job.

Sr. Shirley even had designs to enlarge the small chapel. Her irresistible invitation went out to Msgr. John O'Donnell. He had made a retreat and indicated he wanted to help enlarge the chapel. He had some unallocated cash at his disposal. However, widespread attachment to the present chapel prevented the idea from taking root and his death in 1999 ended her dream at that time.

Financial Acumen

Money continued to be scarce. Scrutinizing the finances, Sister Shirley discovered that the retreat house was paying $16,000 a year in taxes. Really? She decided to have a dinner with a group of lawyers to see what was possibile for a tax exemption. After all, the retreat house was a non-profit religious institution whose sole aim was simply to help people meet God in a prayerful setting. None of the lawyers would touch her proposal. Her blunt response: "I will do it!"

She managed to find a young man working for the Ducharme law firm in Windsor. For a whole year, they worked hard on the proposal which she was writing up. When it could not be presented in the local court at Harrow, she managed to get a venue in Mississauga. Success! She obtained tax exempt status for the retreat house based on its use for education, but they were still going to levy a tax for the parking lot until they were apprised that this was there for their weeping tiles. A cheque soon arrived for back taxes adding up to $48,000. She did it!

It did not take long for her creative spirit, and the ongoing needs of the retreat house, to spend the windfall. "Emmanuel House," a low-slung, fully equipped suite, was added to the north end of Nazareth House. Now retreat masters, and individual retreatants alike, had a superb location to be apart and

Entrance to the addition to Nazareth House

allow the Lord to work in their hearts. The money covered the installation of weeping tile around St. Joseph Building as well as providing for other needs. The Ursuline community paid for renovations to the staff house, where the sisters lived. The three at the retreat house donated their salaries as well to cover the expenses. Expenses continued to pile up, but her vast network of volunteers helped her to stay the costs. Indeed, her policy was that anyone could come to Oxley who needed to pray, even if they could not pay. God would provide. And God did! Bishop Sherlock and his chancellor, Fr. Jim Williams, saw how successfully she was running the retreat house, and repaid her with help from the diocese.

Retreats Abound

Sister Shirley was both an excellent teacher and accomplished in teaching the Catholic faith. She decided to give some of the retreats herself. At first, there was some resistance to her directing men on a retreat. Old attitudes die hard. But a particular retreat to a group of members of the St. Vincent de Paul Society turned the tide. Her new-found skill flourished, much to everyone's benefit. In addition to this new development, Fr. Frank O'Connor, the spiritual director of St. Peter's Seminary, invited her to be one of the retreat directors for the seminarians' annual eight-day retreat held in April. The students loved her. For her, doing retreats was a "beautiful grace." She was "not afraid to enter into another person's bubble." She had a way of unobtrusively asking a retreatant, "How are you doing? What is it that you really need?" Few could resist the inviting love in her eyes and heart.

Seminary Retreat Team (left to right): Fr. Jack O'Flaherty, Sr. Maureen Meloche, Fr. Frank O'Connor, Sr. Shirley, Fr. Prieur, Fr. Mike Michon

Like her predecessors, she too made the rounds of the parishes to invite people to make a retreat. To promote retreats, Sr. Annette, a Holy Name Sister, had prepared a brochure with sketches of the retreat house and surrounding grounds. A variety of retreats was offered. There were retreats for mothers and daughters, Alcoholics Anonymous, abused women as well as for local parishes. The style of the retreats evolved from the "closed" retreats to those that included conferences that were especially based on the scriptures. Following each session, questions were provided for the retreatants to ponder and pray over for a while. Then, retreatants were invited to share the fruits of their reflections in small, voluntary discussion groups. Some of these responses could be brought back to the larger group. Jean Vanier had used this method since the 1970s in his renowned "Faith and Sharing Retreats." Most people loved the combination of silence and voluntary conversation. Fr. Des Scanlon would continue using this method. The retreats at Oxley flourished.

Later, Sr. Loretta Mitchell helped to welcome and greet the various groups from August, 1995 until June, 1997. She handled telephone inquiries, bookings and engaged in hospitality. Cathy Rounding worked in the office for two years, succeeded by Betty Ann McCrindle. We must also mention the names of the great cooks during her tenure: Judy Butera, Cathy Campeau, Anita Corman, Mary Jane Laforet, Sue Malott, Kathy Peters, Judy Wellington, and Wendy Wright. Praying and eating always seem to go better together. Finally, Ron Hamelin kept the grounds in top condition.

Sr. Shirley felt that the diocese lacked a common spirituality. She wanted to show people how they could all have a spiritual life. She emphasized the necessity of asking two questions at the end of every day: (1) What were the *happy* things that happened to me today? (2) What were the *sad* things that happened? This is the Ignatian daily examen of consciousness in miniature. She often urged people not to be afraid of using the word "Jesus," respectfully and unashamedly, in daily conversation. She is convinced that a personal relationship with Jesus will pour out spontaneously from our lips and serve as powerful witness to His presence in our lives.

Sr. Rosie Rau (centre) and a joyful team

I would be quite remiss if I did not highlight the remarkable spirit of Sr. Rose Marie Rau, who was the general *factotum* at the retreat house for seventeen years. Her pleasant smile and eager spirit, her willingness to carry a bag or to find a missing item for a room, all these thousand and one small acts of kindness brought a "special presence" to the retreat house. She typified the wonderful spirit of all the sisters who spent time working at the retreat house. It probably could not have survived without them.

Sr. Shirley ended her tenure in June of 1994. At a deeper level, she shared hat she was gaining a better notion of human weakness in herself and in others. God was teaching her a new degree of dependence on his providence. She humbly admitted that it was her first experience of failure. God has his own ways of bringing us closer to himself.

Yet, her wonderful legacy lives on. She did a remarkable job of refurbishing the retreat house. Throughout it all, she possessed a deep sense of God's joy in her. She had a wonderful, buoyant optimism about what could be done if you put your mind to it. She seemed to take quite literally the Lord's injunction to ask and you will receive (*Matt.* 7:7). Somehow, she could make others dance for joy through her warm and hopeful spirit, her daring leadership, her conferences, her spiritual direction, and her wide group of friends. The statue of the dancing woman which she erected right at the western edge of St. Joseph's Building epitomizes her spirit. It is a powerful symbol of

Dennis and Vicki Ullyett's flowers abound.

what God can do when people come to the retreat house to have their heavy burdens shared and even completely lifted by God. Sr. Shirley remembers that one of the German sisters cooking in their kitchen at the Ursuline House in the west often used to say, "Come happy back!" That line is the last line you see painted on the archway over the sidewalk leading out of the retreat house. Her tenure at Oxley echoed that farewell for countless retreatants.

chapter 9

Fr. Des Scanlan, C.Ss.R.
"The Missionary Educator"

Director from 1994-2008

You like him as soon as you meet him. His welcoming smile and warm handshake capture your heart. This tall, white-haired priest became the sixth director of Holy Family Retreat House in 1994. A cursory look at his life will help us appreciate how he embellished the retreat movement during his fourteen-year tenure.

A Montrealer in Ontario

The eldest of five children, Desmond Scanlan was born on June 8, 1932, in Montréal and grew up in the city's Point St. Charles area. He was educated at Canon O'Meara Academy and Loyola High School before attending three years at the Redemptorist juvenate, St. Mary's College, Brockville, where he graduated in 1952. Entering the Redemptorist Novitiate at L'Abord à Plouffe, Québec, he professed first vows on September 15, 1953.

He began his theological and philosophical studies at St. Alphonsus Seminary in Woodstock, Ontario, and continued theological studies at the newly opened Redemptorist seminary of Holy Redeemer College in Windsor. A member of the first ordination class at Holy Redeemer College, he was ordained on June 22, 1958, by Bishop John Christopher Cody of London. While assisting at St. Alphonsus parish in Windsor, he earned a Bachelor of Arts degree at Assumption University of Windsor in 1960. During his appointment as a teacher at St. Mary's College (1960–1965), Fr. Scanlan received his permanent teacher's certificate in 1963 after studying during the summers.

Returning to Holy Redeemer College, Fr. Scanlan, whom everyone calls "Fr. Des," held positions as Prefect of Students (1965–1966) and Rector (1966–1975). During this time, he earned a Master of Arts degree in education (1968) from Villanova University, Villanova, Pennsylvania, and served as a religion consultant for the Windsor Roman Catholic Separate Schoo: Board (1971–1982). At the University of Windsor, he was also an instructor in summer courses in catechetics (1972–1974, 1978–1980) and sessional instructor in religious education (1980–1982). At the Windsor Teachers' College, he was an instructor in religion (1972–1978). He received a specialist religious education certificate (1981) from the Ontario English Catholic Teachers' Association.

In 1982, he was appointed to Toronto as director of the Redemptorist Formation Program and continued with this assignment throughout his three terms as Provincial Superior of the Redemptorists' Toronto Province, to which he was first elected in 1984. After retiring as Provincial Superior in 1993, he joined the staff at Holy Family Retreat House, becoming director in 1994 and retiring in June 2008.

Transition to the Retreat House

Having retired as Provincial Superior in 1993, Fr. Des came to the retreat house as chaplain, for a "working sabbatical," in August of that year. Sr. Shirley described herself as the "Executive Director." He spent the next year working alongside her, celebrating the sacraments and preaching retreats. During Lent of 1994, Sr. Shirley resigned as director, feeling her time had come. Reluctantly, Bishop Sherlock finally accepted her second attempt to step down. Another era had ended.

Bishop Sherlock wanted to make Fr. Des the "Interim Director." Fr. Ray Corriveau, the Redemptorist superior, visited Windsor and the appointment came alive. However, the bishop intuitively sensed Fr. Des's talents, and called him in November to name him "Director." He accepted. Fr. Corriveau snuffed: "I should never have agreed to 'Interim'!" But the deed was done.

Needless to say, it was an ideal appointment. His rich experience in teaching, spirituality, religious education, training seminarians and directing retreats all converged as he took on this new post. As we have seen over and over again, the Holy Spirit has an amazing way of discovering needed talents "just in time." How modern!

Resuming the Pace

Fr. Des has energy. He is a consummate storyteller, using his rich bass voice to enthrall an audience. His Redemptorist preaching style knows how to command immediate attention. He can adapt to young and old alike. The glint in his eye leads people into the joy of knowing GOD. He had managed to slough off the "hellfire-and-brimstone" tone of the more traditional Redemptorist retreat mode. St. Alphonsus would be proud of his adaptation.

Sr. Shirley had embedded even more deeply the wonderful ethos of the retreat house: all-pervasive hospitality, an ecumenical and interfaith attitude, and a Catholic inclusivity for a multitude of spiritual approaches to prayer and human needs. The die was cast for Fr. Des.

Merry Christmas 2005

Fr. Jansen had left a deep legacy of offering retreats for Grade 8 and high school students and had insisted that their teachers sit in on the presentations. Fr. Des followed suit. He continued to have two women's retreats every year along with one for men and one for the Vincentians, the members of the St. Vincent de Paul Society, as well as a directed retreat for religious women. Some parishes managed to come for a weekend retreat. Fr. Dan Morand, pastor of the French parish of St. Jérôme in Windsor, would get a preacher from Québec, and his parish attendance for these retreats soon went from forty to sixty and more. The retired Sisters of the Immaculate Heart of Mary Community in Detroit came for both preached and directed retreats. Other religious women came for preached retreats.

Rick Farias, the chaplain at Villanova High School, would bring out his youth group and ask Fr. Des to celebrate "Sunrise Masses on the beach." Why not! He would oblige, and the death and resurrection of Jesus became a new reality for them.

The Jesuit-run University of Detroit High School had a long tradition of coming to Oxley. They even stayed overnight, expanding from one night to two. One of their organizations was "Kairos," and they would sometimes stay from Tuesday to Friday. Fr. Des complimented them for their wonderful openness and sacramental celebrations, acknowledging the excellent preparation and training the Jesuits had done for them. Fr. C. Rice, S.J., was one of their pioneers in this annual trek to the northern shores of Lake Erie.

Another Jesuit-run location in inner-city Detroit, namely Loyola House, also came to Oxley. These rough and ready teenagers had a rocky beginning at the tranquil retreat house site. But Fr. Des was convinced that these adolescents—often poor or abandoned—deserved a second chance at Oxley, since their quite tumultuous maiden voyage was probably the first time they had ever been to any location with so much quiet. They kept coming back.

The University of Detroit Jesuits also came for days of reflection to prepare for their students' retreats. Loyola House imitated this very fruitful practice.

The Retreats Thrive

Fr. Des loved to help with the pastoral needs of some local parishes, especially St. Anthony parish in Harrow. He would pitch in at the retreat house when there was a parish retreat from St. John the Baptist parish in Amherstburg.

Many full retreats continued to be offered for various groups of Alcoholics Anonymous (AA), especially some from the United States. They were known as "The Oxley AA." Some retreatants were HIV-positive and were welcome to attend. The "inclusivity" dimension remains quite evident. In addition, student nurses would come to Oxley for spiritual refreshment. All this needed much patient priming and encouragement.

Of course, the annual eight-day directed retreat for the students of St. Peter's Seminary at the end of April continued year after year with great success. Started in 1974, this annual eight-day retreat plunged the retreat centre into a kind of "deep silence," not even allowing for any "knowing glances," as forbidden by Msgr. Pat Cavanagh in his annual "Keep the Silence Talk." The cooks loved this retreat: they could cook "real meals," compared to the hot dog, fries and pizzas so dear to the teenage clientele. The uproarious "talking breakfast" on the eighth day, after remarkable "retreat words" or graces had been shared after communion at Mass, seemed to make up for all the silence of the previous week. More amazing graces![1]

Maintaining the Retreat House

Sr. Shirley's legacy of a well-run and well-kept retreat house carried on. "Gates" continued to perform his carpenter wizardry for the retreat house. Mr. Gauthier's carpenter and roofing business maintained dry quarters for everyone. Wendy Wright, Anita Corman and Cathy Campeau—the three cooks—made sure that no one went home hungry. Betty Ann McCrindle retired from teaching and did wonderful administrative work. Sr. Rosie Rau, O.S.U., exuded her ever-present aura of joy and endless service for whatever was needed. Ron Hamelin made sure the grounds were well kept and the birds undisturbed in their annual spring nesting locations.

---

1 For a more detailed account of the history of these retreats, see Michael Prieur, "Come away and I will refresh you," *The Alumni Bulletin of St. Peter's Seminary*, No. 51, December, 1991, 53–54.

Fr. Des loves to indicate how people, searching for the location of the retreat house while driving through Harrow, just got the response: "It's out here somewhere."[2]

The wonderful retreat team with Fr. Des

In reverse, Fr. Des took pride and interest in being part of the Harrow and surrounding communities. He enjoyed the pleasant staff at local stores and other businesses with whom he dealt as he contributed to the local economy. The men and women who carried out the services offered by the retreat house were local residents.

Thoughts on Holy Family's Future

Fr. Des is firm on this: "Don't lose Oxley!" This spiritual oasis is necessary more than ever in our hectic world. The numbers are down, true, but so is church attendance. People coming from

Fr. Des and friends

the London end of the diocese are on the decline. A fresh P.R. group for them is needed. He would like to see more participants from King's University College in London. The retreat house needs to bring in a constant stream of fresh preachers and new groups of retreatants. Parish priests need to see retreats for

---

2   See Fr. Des Scanlan, "Holy Family Retreat House—'Out There Somewhere,'" *The Harrow News*, February 3, 1998, 5.

their parishioners, *not* as an infringement on their pastoral ministry, but as enrichment for their parishes. Retreats are a win/win engagement for the parish and the retreat house. Also, groups for retreats need to be cultivated from other locales like Ohio, as well as various parish groups like the Catholic Women's League.

Fr. Des likes to quote Bishop Sherlock's designation for the retreat house, which he enunciated at the fiftieth anniversary celebration: "Holy Family Retreat House is a place of compassion for the needs of the people of the Diocese." Elaborating on this, Fr. Des says that retreats are a place where people struggling with their marriages can get a "different read" on their circumstances, compared to what the parish can give them. For Jewish people, Oxley can be a true "Sabbath" location for a day of rest. It is a place where people who feel rejected—for AA and HIV-positive people, as well as people "with dirty laundry"—can be assuaged and encouraged.

Fr. Des truly exemplified the deep charismas of hospitality, inclusivity, and compassion so deeply embedded in Holy Family Retreat House. When he officially retired in June 2008, a tangible emptiness pervaded this holy ground. But his willingness to support the new leadership in any way possible is a tribute to this compassionate, gentle, and gracious Redemptorist. The parish of St. John the Baptist in Amherstburg, where he is now retired, is the true beneficiary of this preaching giant and son of St. Alphonsus Liguori.

Affirmations

May 24 - 07

Oh the wonder of this place - The beauty, the peace, the friendliness, and yes the solitude if you so desire. Solitude - but never alone! For wherever you walk on these Holy Grounds or whatever building you are in, God is there, he is there in the TRINITY -

The Father - who watches over us and give caring advice

The Son - He is like a

brother to me, ready to guide and be companion

The Holy Spirit - Enlightens me to be open to all the graces - so freely given if we believe.

And all of the creation that

surrounds us, without the bustling interruptions of normal life in this year of 2007. The beautiful waters, oh how I love gazing at these waters. This morning the lake is just quietly rippling at other times it has been roaring waves, just as our lives ebb and flow! The sky, the sunshine, the clouds; the nature in trees so full of life at this time of year with nesting birds – feeding their young. The grounds abound with beauty!

The kindness of all who work here – and, the smiling nod of other retreatants; all so respectful of one another – conversation if wanted or needed; silence if so desired. Every nook + corner has its special calling – and now dear reader the chapel is calling me for a moment with my Lord. This visit truly has relaxed and renewed me in Body, Mind, and Spirit.

May you always be equally blest.

M.D.

May 25 – 2009

Thanks to Almighty God of this wonderful peace Holy Family Retreat It has provided the peace rest and comfort we all of us once again this trip. We have each found our own solace and spent time with the Lord.

The awesome soothing waves the sweet sound of birds, the subtle breeze, the beautiful places to rest awhile, to be quiet is to be in discussion – your choice.

The most wonderful staff – everyone of them so anxious to please & do anything to make your stay here perfect.

It is certainly a place of restoration – meeting old and new friends, spending time together, eating and yes laughing.

Thank you Lord for this wonderful provision

We Love You.

W.H.

Bishop J.M. Sherlock with (left to right) Fr. Jansen, Fr. Gatfield, and Fr. Meloche

The Knights of Columbus, faithful supporters from the beginning

Music in abundance

Friends, new and old

Fr. Meloche, ever the preacher

It always tastes better at the lake.

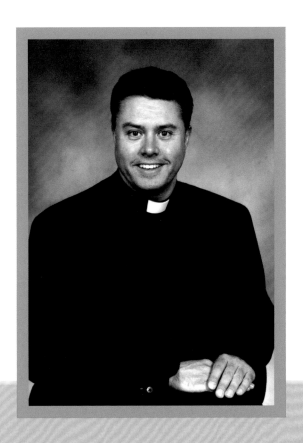

chapter 10

Fr. Gary Ducharme
"New Dreams and Hopes"

Director from 2008–2010

He has a hopeful face with a sparkle in his eyes. He moves about the retreat grounds with a relaxed manner, frequently breaking out with a warm smile. He makes you feel at home. Fr. Gary wanted a change from parish ministry. His parishioners loved him. He also loves the spiritual life. All this is a great recipe for someone to replace the wonderfully wise and popular Fr. Scanlan.

We present the pastoral ministry of Fr. Gary Ducharme. He was baptized at St. Boniface Church in Zurich, Ontario, the son of Gerard and Mary Ducharme. His early schooling was at St. Joseph, Ontario as well as the public high school in Exeter, Ontario. He obtained his B.A. and M.Div. from St. Peter's Seminary, being ordained by Bishop J.M. Sherlock on May 7, 1983 in St. Peter's Cathedral.

Pastorally, he served in Windsor, London, Lucan, Bothwell and Glencoe, and Bright's Grove. He took Part One of the Internship in Ignatian Spirituality from the Manresa Jesuit Retreat House in Detroit, Michigan. He also did a Summer Practicum in Spirituality with the Jesuits at Loyola House in Guelph, Ontario in 2008. His contact with the retreat house began in the summer of 1977 as a first-year seminarian. Along with other students, he helped as a host in the kitchen. There, he met Fr. Jansen for the first time. Few people "met" Fr. Jansen without experiencing his love of God and Catholicity in spades! This influence continued as Fr. Gary spent two summers as a seminarian living with Fr. Percy Drouillard, Fr. Jansen's classmate. As a priest, Fr. Ducharme enjoyed being in the same support group with Fr. Rocheleau while he was the director of the retreat house. We should note that Fr. Ducharme made the most of his annual, end-of-year seminarian retreats at Oxley. These eight-day, personally directed retreats deeply marked both his own spirituality and his love for the retreat centre.

He had also encountered Sr. Shirley McAuley, O.S.U., at the Renewal Centre in Windsor. Later, during the first year of her directorship of the retreat house, he was "invited" to give his first retreat to a group from the St. Vincent de Paul Society. He noted that, as we have experienced earlier, Sr. Shirley has a "persuasive way." It was a great experience for him.

All these providential events seemed to insert a strong pull inside Fr. Gary to be more involved with the retreat house. It did not take much convincing for him to respond to the diocesan leadership's request for him to succeed Fr. Scanlan. Again, a fresh broom was now at the welcoming door in St. Mary's Building.

Fr. Gary is someone who is both sensitive to the times and overflowing with hopes for the future. He envisages a "Spiritual and Pastoral Program Committee." He is anxious to address some key concerns: everyone's weekends are extremely busy; retirees and seniors have lots of weekday time on their hands; a few diocesan reviews surfaced concerns about a certain spiritual neglect due to the overload in the lives of diocesan personnel and/or parishioners; there is a growing need for more outside groups to come to Oxley.

The list could be almost endless. The fundamental question is simple: the retreat house is definitely a spiritual oasis available to the diocese and ready to respond to the first category of the newly minted Diocesan Pastoral Plan, namely, the call to holiness for everyone. This call could be addressed, in part, by possibly providing something that high schools cannot produce for their students in any consistent manner: a quiet venue. The need could also be met by working with youth coordinators in the diocese. Indeed, there is a long tradition at Oxley of doing such work for young people and their leaders.

Fr. Ducharme's hopes for the future continue. Could the retreat house become a centre of spirituality for priests? These men continue to long for a deeper spirituality, and some even for a thirty-day Ignatian retreat. As well, parish pastoral teams yearn for spiritual support for the incessant demands and pastoral pressures that come their way. He also envisages picking up on previous directors' "Road Shows," whereby they went out to the parishes (on weekends or at parish events) to promote retreats at the retreat house.

The inauguration of the Institute for Catholic Formation, which is allied to St. Peter's Seminary, presented a new challenge for the retreat house, which has become more directly associated with them. This entailed a fresh restructuring of job descriptions for the lay staff, with the consequent loss of many individuals and a hiring of new personnel. This was necessitated by both the need for more focused work plans and responding to ever-increasing financial constraints. It was all very painful, but necessary.

Fr. Ducharme wanted to restructure the advisory board. While giving credit to their fine contributions in the past, he nevertheless envisaged deeper connections with the Board of Directors and its four committees: (1) finances; (2) buildings and property; (3) development and fund-raising; and, (4) pastoral and spiritual programming. The theme of "stewardship" punctuated his remarks. The never-ending challenge to achieve financial self-sufficiency was never far from the door. He was most appreciative to Bishop Bill McGrattan (then-rector of St. Peter's Seminary), Maria Serodio-Teves, the seminary food services manager, and Fr. Gerard Dewan, a seminary faculty member with extensive financial background, all of whom had helped him with these many transitions.

Hope for the Future

Fr. Gary's face lights up when he speaks about the youth of today. He mentioned a retreat for students of King's University College in January 2008, which he said was somewhat typical for young people coming here. While many seemed to lack a current connection to their parishes, nevertheless they all exhibited a deep spiritual hunger for God and for deepening their faith-life. They all said they could feel the holiness present in the very atmosphere of the retreat house. He noted that often, when adults were at Oxley, they remained "noisy," while young people remained more "reverent." They willingly abandoned their iPods and computers. They made excellent confessions. And they were benefitting from good youth facilitators who seemed to have shifted from just "doing ministry" and preaching to them, to being positive supporters and witnesses to the faith in a team approach. This bodes well for the future.

Fr. Ducharme would love to see the retreat house help people to "catch fire" with God. He yearns to see people coming from all age levels and from all parts of the diocese and even from Michigan. He is very open to being a part of this ever-old, yet ever new, spiritual thrust here at Oxley. He truly believes that the charism of Holy Family Retreat House is that of "Holy Ground," alluding to the sign over the archway at the entrance, "You are standing on Holy Ground." He is most direct: "People meet God here face to face." Judging from his deep faith and personal enthusiasm, it is easy to see why God would respond to this dream. Again, the retreat house saga continues.

Postscript

The 2010 spring moves of the London diocese brought more changes to the retreat house. Fr. Ducharme realized that he missed parish ministry more than he had anticipated when he began at the retreat house. Accordingly, he has been assigned as pastor to St. Peter's parish in Goderich, just "up the road" from where he was born in the "French Settlement." Bishop Fabbro has appointed Deacon Paul Giroux as the administrator of the retreat house.

Fr. Michael O'Brien, newly retired, now lives in the house and provides sacramental ministry to any retreatants. Both of these men bring a wealth of experience from their administration of the diocesan shrine at St. Patrick's parish in Merlin,

Another happy retreat ending...with Fr. Mike O'Brien as the celebrant of the Mass (2010)

Ontario for the past five years or so. The bishop has appointed a "Vision Committee" to examine options for the future of the retreat house. Once again, Holy Family Retreat House is in need of a "fresh broom" and new dreams to continue providing a peaceful venue to listen to God's Spirit.

Affirmations

April 11, 2008

I was sitting here and I saw this book. I guess my only advice is to cherish those you hold dear. Although I don't know you, I'll pray for you. I wish you the best and hope you will come closer to God as I have.

I wrote this poem in this exact place and I hope it means something to you.

> *The wind moves across my neck*
> *it is slow, it is meek*
> *the puddle splashes at my feet*

once again, it feels sweet

To know these simple things
to wait and stop just hear
and silent voice cry out
just to hold them dear

You gotta stop and listen, hear
just stop and stay where you are
He is here, He is new
He really ain't that far.

Let Him brush your cheek
let Him wash your feet
and soon you'll know and see
all of this, this sweet beauty

These trees show your face
Comfort me and feel safe
three rocks let me sit
my pain, I don't know it.

I wish I could see all of this
I wish I just knew how
to live and love and cherish you
but instead I put you down

You gotta stop and listen, hear
just stop and stay where you are
He is here, He is near
He really ain't that far.

Let him show his face
Sit in this holy space
and soon, you'll know and see
all of this, His sweet beauty

You gotta stop and listen hear
just stop and stay where you are
He is here, He is near
He really ain't that far.

Just stop and listen here
He is here, He is near
Love in Him, and Love them so
Just to hold him dear.

I love you,
M.K.

epilogue

W hen preparing a homily or sermon, preachers are instructed to follow these guidelines: "Say what are you going to say, say it, and then, say what you have said." Epilogues do the last of the three.

As the subject indicates, the laity often spearheaded the "Lay Retreat Movement" in our diocese, and indeed in North America. Priests go on retreat for at least five days every year. Why should the laity not do something similar, even if only for a briefer time? Everyone needs time to "go apart, pray and reflect on what really matters," the root meaning of "retreat" when used spiritually. This means to stop, look and listen, especially with a lot of *silence,* which is the language of God.

Some prayerful priests, bishops and even a Pope galvanized this powerful movement of the Spirit. They articulated the vital connection between prayer and any Catholic action or social change. The message is right out of the gospel: Jesus himself made such a connection in his ministry on earth, frequently going away alone to a "lonely place" to pray. The movement was truly inclusive. It embraced men and women, young and old, Catholic, Jewish, many other faiths, and especially individuals with profound personal struggles. God's kingdom includes everyone.

The "Retreat Movement" was sown and germinated in our own diocese in various institutional venues like the seminary as well as Catholic university and religious settings at both ends of the diocese. Highly talented and even prophetic individuals emerged at the behest of our church leaders, to provide retreats for the hearts of many individuals. Once begun, countless volunteers came out of the woodwork to maintain the daring venture of Holy Family Retreat House with untold hours of self-sacrificing generosity. Consecrated religious women with extraordinarily generous hearts were especially evident in the whole picture. The lay staff exhibited memorable concern for the retreatants. The retreat house was always run "on a shoestring," as the saying goes. Evangelical poverty and begging seemed to be its lot. But God always delivered. Interestingly enough, times of tension and threatened extinction seemed to be catalysts for the next surge of spiritual energy to propel the retreat house forward for another generation.

It must be mentioned that retreats thrived in our diocese in other venues concurrent to the history of Holy Family Retreat House. A huge debt of gratitude is owed to the Spirit-filled individuals who ran places like St. Mary's Academy (now gone, sad to say), Assumption College (in earlier days), Brescia Hall, St. Peter's Seminary, Medaille House in London, the Redemptorist House in Woodstock, Ontario, Port Burwell, Precious Blood Monastery and the Michaelite House in Melrose, Ontario, just west of London. Not to be forgotten are the countless days of prayer at innumerable sites which happen all over the diocese each year for every level of diocesan and parish grouping. This could be the subject of another book.

It is also amazing how St. Peter's Seminary has been such a constant thread in the tapestry of the lay retreat movement in our diocese. Its prayerful daily schedule as well as numerous dedicated alumni, who were essential ingredients at the retreat house, made the seminary in London the godfather for the "Seminary of the Laity" in Oxley. The connection continues to be renewed to this day.

But the nub of all this is our universal need for prayer and quiet reflection. St. Cyril of Jerusalem deftly indicates what can happen: "The Spirit comes gently and makes himself known by his fragrance. He is not felt as a burden, for he is light, very light."[1] The Spirit comes light as a feather, a whiff of a sweet scent, a tug in the heart. This happens to everyone. Our problem is that we are so frazzled and overwhelmed with noisy activity that we cannot discern these subtle movements of the Spirit. But they are constantly present in our hearts.

It is my deepest hope that this small work will be a gentle nudge for all its readers to pause, and simply ask the question, "When was the last time that I truly shut down and made a silent retreat?" Indeed, there are still many retreat centres simply waiting for your phone call. "Holy Ground" awaits us all.

---

1   *The Liturgy of the Hours*, Vol. 2, 968.

Staff Picture, Holy Family Retreat House, April 20, 2011

Left to right: Len Mayea, Maintenance; Helen Chartier, Housekeeper; Chantale Bouchard, Chef; Erin Bechard, Chef; Deacon Paul Giroux, Interim Director; Fr. Michael O'Brien, Priest in Residence. Absent: Mary Salmon, Assistant to the Director

appendices

Appendix 1: Stations of the Cross

Station I   The plaque is missing.

Station II

GIFT OF SIR HARRY E. GIGNAC K.S.G
IN HONOR OF
THE HOLY FAMILY

Station III

GIFT
MR & MRS L.L. ODETTE

Station IV

GIFT
OF THE FAMILY
IN MEMORY OF
FT. LT. JAMES E. SHERRY

Station V

GIFT
ANTHONY COLAUTTI

Station VI

GIFT
ANTHONY COLAUTTI

Station VII

GIFT
T.J. SEGUIN
IN MEMORY OF WIFE
MARIE ROSE SEGUIN

Station VIII

GIFT
JOHN WALL

Station IX

GIFT
H.J. MCMANUS
IN MEMORY OF HIS FATHER

Station X

GIFT
JOHN REDDICK
IN MEMORY OF
BRUCE AND MAUDE REDDICK

Station XI   The plaque is missing.

Station XII

GIFT
LEO PAGE
"FATHER OF RETREATS"

Station XIII

DONATED BY
MR & MRS DOLPHIS J. KNAPP
& FAMILY
IN MEMORY OF THE LATE
MR & MRS URLIC KNAPP, SR.

Station XIV

GIFT OF SIR HARRY E. GIGNAC, K.S.G.
IN MEMORY OF HIS MOTHER AND FATHER
MR. & MRS. ALFRED GIGNAC

Appendix 2: Brother Knights on Retreat Board (1949)

Most Reverend John T. Kidd, D.D., Bishop of London, announced the names of the Retreat Board of Directors at the annual dinner of the Retreat League.

It is interesting to note that all, (with the exception of one or two), are members of the Knights of Columbus.

We wish to congratulate these members for the honour bestowed upon them. We feel sure that under the guidance and protection of the Holy Family, the Retreat House at Oxley will progress in every way.

The following are the names: Rev. Arthur Meloche, spiritual director; Sir Harry Gignac, K.S.G., president; Right Reverend Wilfrid J. Langlois, D.P., V.F., and Leo Page, honorary presidents; George Hanrahan, vice-president; F. S. Arbour, secretary-treasurer.

Organization Committee:	George Janisse, Rev. G.L. Blonde, Philip J. Waters, and George O'Rourke.
Promotion Committee:	Desire Gemus, Rev. I.J.Poisson, Truman Dillon, and Howard J. Pray.
Personnel Committee:	Frank Clarke, Rev. J.A. Roney, A.F. Fuerth, and Clifford P. Marancie.
Maintenance Committee:	G.W. Cronk, Rev. G. Pitre, G.J. Petz, and Antonio Colautti.
Finance Committee:	John Wall, Rev. Walsh, Col. Paul Poisson, M.C., V.D., and R.J. Desmarais.

Ref.: "Brother Knights on Retreat Board," *Knights of Columbus Bulletin*, Vol. 25, Jan. 1949.

Appendix 3: "The Holy Family in the Carpenter Shop"

The renowned artist, Philip Aziz, had just finished his schooling at Yale University when Bishop John Christopher Cody, the bishop of London, commissioned him to do a painting in honour of the Holy Family. It was 1948, and the Retreat House had just been opened. It was one of his first paintings. For years, the painting resided on the wall of the small dining room in St. Mary's building. Only recently has it been moved to the artist's home in London for safe keeping in the light of impending work on the building along with possible refurbishing of some parts damaged over the years.

The artist himself wrote the following "Note" on the back of the painting:

"This painting 'The Holy Family in the Carpenter Shop' is a commission given to me by His Excellency Bishop Coty (sic), of London, Canada – completed this day – Dec. 18, 1948.
–   Tempera on masonite gessoed surface ultramarine and lapis lazuli in blue of the virgin's robe.
–   Do not touch painted surface with hands, or cloth damp or otherwise
–   Varnish will take place two years from this date."

(Signed) Philip J. Aziz

Painted on three sides of the black frame in gold letters, all very hard to read due to the deterioration of the paint, is a citation from the New Testament: *Venite ad me omnes, qui laboratis, et onerati estis, et ego reficiam vos.* Matt. XI, XXVIII. ("Come to me all you who labour and are overburdened, and I will refresh you." *Mt.* 11:28) On the bottom of the frame is the date when it was done: MDCCCCXLVIII.

Philip Aziz was Lebanese by nationality. He had deep Christian faith through his Greek Orthodox roots. His theology, shown through many of his religious paintings is remarkable. His greatest interpreter was Fr. Anthony Durand, a long-time professor at St. Peter's Seminary in London. Fr. Durand would often pronounce that "He doesn't even know what he is painting! It is his artistic genius that is speaking through his art." Worth considering.

Jesus's right hand is poised in the classic position of one speaking with divine authority. The single rose is, in essence, the symbol of completion, of consummate completion and perfection. The pomegranate, due to "its shape and internal structure rather than from its colour, is the reconciliation of the multiple and diverse within apparent unity. Hence, in the Bible, for example, it appears as a symbol of the Oneness of the universe. It is also symbolic of fecundity."[1] Rose and pomegranate speak powerfully of the perfect and unique

---

1   J.E. Cirlot, *A Dictionary of Symbols*, N.Y., Philosophical Library, 1962, p. 249.

role of the Christ-child. The handsaw on the wall indicates Joseph's trade. Could the crutch bespeak Joseph's aging condition? On the bottom of Mary's blue dress is painted *Mater amabilis Regina Coeli*, Beloved Mother, Queen of Heaven. I leave it to the reader/viewer to interpret the focus of the eyes of Joseph, Mary and Jesus.

I thank Fr. Michael O'Brien, Deacon Paul Giroux, and Barry Callow, the long-time friend and artistic associate of Philip Aziz, for their solicitous help in providing for the recent care of this masterpiece, and Ellie Lagrandeur, extolled by Philip Aziz for her artistic qualities.

A Masterpiece in Progress

Unveiling the painting, Prince Edward Hotel, 1948

Appendix 4: Holy Family Retreat House brochure (1967)

This is the 1967 Schedule for the retreats being held at the retreat house. It is amazing how many different groups wended their way to Oxley in those days. The number of contact persons in each parish or organization pays tribute to the organizational skills of Frs. Meloche and Gatfield in this era. Making their phone numbers available on the brochure (blacked out here) shows how willing they were to be called to arrange for a retreat. How times have changed!

Holy Family

Retreat House
for the
Service
of the
Community

1967

retreats   retraites
days of renewal   recollections
seminars   journées d'études

(OXLEY) R.R. No. 1, HARROW, ONTARIO
TELEPHONE 738-4243

1967 SCHEDULE

JANUARY

8   Retreat Leaders meeting at University
     Centre, Windsor

10-12 STUDENTS

13-15 STUDENTS

20-22 MARRIED COUPLES
     Organizers: Mr. & Mrs. A. Robinet ....

23-25 STUDENTS

27-29 STUDENTS

30-2 Students

FEBRUARY

7-9 STUDENTS

10-12 REGIS CLUBS OF THE DIOCESE
     Chaplain: Rev. T. J. Lever ....

14-16 STUDENTS

17-19 Y. C. W. AND UNIVERSITY STUDENTS
     (Girls)

22   DAY OF RENEWAL FOR CLERGY

24-26 Y. C. W. AND UNIVERSITY STUDENTS
     (Girls)

28-2 STUDENTS

MARCH

3-5 BOYS OF ALL PARISHES (Age 16 to 18)
     Chaplain: Rev. N. McGillis ....

10-12 MEN
     Chaplain: Rev. J. M. Williams ....
     Organizer: Mr. T. Daigneau ....
     Leader:
     Chatham: B. Sacrament: Mr. N. Belanger ....
     Chatham: St. Joseph: Mr. G. Sans ....
     Chatham: St. Ursula: Mr. M. Charlevoix ....
     Chatham: St. Anthony: Mr. S. Stirling ......
     Chatham: St. Agnes: Mr. J. Lacina ....
     Merlin: Mr. H. Dillon ....
     Blenheim: Mr. J. Huys ....
     Prairie Siding: Mr. F. Bruette ....
     Dresden: Mr. J. Caron ....
     Ridgetown: Mr. H. Vandergriendt ....
     Tilbury: Mr. A. Gaudreau ....

14-16 STUDENTS

17-19 ENGAGED COUPLES
     Chaplain: Rev. R. Janisse, CSB ....

23-25 GIRLS OF ALL PARISHES (age 16 to 18)

28-30 GIRLS OF ALL PARISHES (age 16 to 18)

31-2 **MEN**
     Chaplain: Rev. C. W. Janisse ....
     Organizer: Mr. W. Green ....
     Christ the King: Mr. B. Rondot, Leader ......
     St. Gabriel: Mr. J. Reaume ....
     St. Martin de Porres: Mr. R. Janisse ....
     O. L. of Mt. Carmel: Mr. F. Smith ....
     Assumption: Mr. A. Lopes ....

APRIL

3-6 STUDY DAYS FOR PREACHERS

7-9 WOMEN
     Chaplain: Rt. Rev. J . Uyen, D.P. ....
     Organizer: Mrs. M. O'Neil ....
     St. Anthony: Miss F. Gazarek, leader ....
     St. Joseph: Miss D. Kouyzer ....
     St. Ursula: Mrs. P. Curry ....
     B. Sacrament: Mrs. M. Ashton ....
     St. Agnes: Mrs. S. Robert ....
     Stevenson: Mrs. L. Benoit .... Wheatley
     Tilbury: Mrs. R. Smith ....

14-16 WOMEN
     Chaplain: Rev. J. O'Donnell ....
     Organizer: Mrs. M. O'Neil ....
     Wallaceburg
     O. L. Help of C; Mrs. L. Lauwereys leader ..
     Holy Family Mrs. M. Coveny ....
     Ridgetown: Mrs. H. Vandergriendt ....
     Dresden: Mrs. G. Tacq ....
     Thamesville: Mrs. D. Culnan ....
     Big Point: Mrs. F. Cadotte ....
     Blenheim: Mrs. M. Perrault ....
     Merlin: Mrs. M. Irwin ....

21-23 MEN
     Chaplain: Rev. C. McNabb ....
     Organizer: Mr. G. Lapierre ....
     Sacred Heart: Mr. J. Hatnean, leader ....
     Sacred Heart: Mr. G. McTavish ....
     St. John Vianney: Mr. T. Prieur ....
     O.L. of Fatima: Mr. L. Ouellette ....
     St. Theresa: Mr. J. Sobocan ....
     St. Thomas: Mr. V. Sobocan ....
     St. Rose: Mr. W. Quinn ....
     St. Anthony: Mr. M. Fedich ....

MAY

5-7 WOMEN
     Chaplain: Rev. T. J. McReavy, CSB ....
     Organizer: Mrs. R. Walker ....
     Holy Name: Mrs. N. Gagnier ....
     B. Sacrament: Mrs. B. Menard ....
     Assumption: Mrs. K. Bagley ....
     St. Patrick: Mrs. J. Phillips ....
     St. Paul: Mrs. G. Renaud ....

12-14 RETREAT FOR A.A.
     Chaplain: Rev. P. Charbonneau ....
     Leader: Mr. F. Brannagan ....

19-21 MARRIED COUPLES
     Chaplain: Rev. F. J. McCarty CSB ....
     Leaders: Mr. & Mrs. A. Robinet ....

23-25 LADIES OF ALL PARISHES (Mid-week)
Chaplain: Rev. S. A. Nouvion
Organizer: Mrs. R. Walker
Leader: Mrs. J. F. Venney

26-28 MEN
Chaplain: Rev. F. J. Walsh
Organizer: Mr. J. Sobocan
St. Clare: Mr. C. Vargas, leader
St. Clare: Mr. W. Bedard
St. Alphonsus: Mr. B. O'Connell
I.C.C.: Mr. G. Belanger
St. Anne: Mr. D. Leeder
St. Christopher: Mr. A. Drouillard
O.L. of Perpetual Help: Mr. J. Robinet
St. Angela: Mr. J. Pizzinato

JUNE

2-4 WOMEN
Chaplain: Rev. J. E. Martin CSB
Organizer: Mrs. T. Daigneau
Amherstburg: Mrs. J. Gignac, leader
Maidstone: Mrs. E. Milligan
Woodslee: Mrs. R. Bissonnette .... Pl. Pk.
Essex: Mrs. R. Kaake
Harrow: Mrs. C. Langlois
Kingsville: Miss F. Kwasnycia
Leamington: Mrs. T. Girard
Wheatley: Mrs. A. Dust

5-9 RETREAT FOR PRIESTS

9-11 WOMEN
Chaplain: Rev. A. Sillery, M.S.
Organizer: Mrs. P. Goyeau
St. Rose: Mrs. R. Oleynik
O. L. of the Rosary: Mrs. S. Alexander
O.L. of Guadalupe: Mrs. H. Menard
St. John Vianney: Mrs. J. Renaud
O.L. of Fatima: Mrs. V. Morand
St. Gregory: Mrs. E. Balogh
St. Thomas: Mrs. R. Schmidt

16-18 WOMEN
Chaplain: Rev. F. M. Doll
Organizer: Mrs. E. J. Boutette
Emeryville: Mrs. R. Seguin, leader
Tecumseh: Mrs. J. Marcotte
LaSalle: Mrs. F. Cash
River Canard: Mrs. E. Anderson
McGregor: Mrs. L. Lucier
Belle River: Miss P. Sauve 70-R-2
Staples: Mrs. J. Bauer .... Woods. 15-11
Comber: Mrs. D. Price .... Woods. 61-R-25

19-23 GRADE 8 DAYS OF RENEWAL

23-25 GERMAN SPEAKING LADIES
Chaplain: V. .Rev. C. Moullion, P.C.
Leader: Mrs. A. Beck

26-30 GRADE 8 DAYS OF RENEWAL

JULY

7-9 LES DAMES HORS DE LA VILLE DE WINDSOR
Aumonier: M. l'Abbe L. H. Rivard 26-R-2
Organizateur: Mlle. Cecile Beneteau
Chef: Mlle. C. Durocher BR-330-R-6

11-13 LES DAMES DE LA VILLE DE WINDSOR (milieu de semaine)
Aumonier: M. l'Abbe O. Martin
Organizateur: Mlle. Cecile Beneteau
Chef: Mme.. G. Guay

14-16 ST. VINCENT DE PAUL SOCIETY
Chaplain: Rev. A. P. Marentette 26-R-2
Leader: Mr. J. Benoit

21-23 WOMEN
Chaplain: Rev. H. R. Reardon
Organizer: Miss Ann Drouillard
St. Joseph: Miss M. Butnari
St. Joseph: Mrs. W. Galarneau
Precious Blood: Mrs. L. Perrault
St. Theresa: Mrs. J. McCartney
St. Vincent de Paul: Mrs. Wm. Strelczyk
O.L. of Perpetual Help: Mrs. E. Bellemore
St. Christopher: Miss Wilma Gelinas

AUGUST

5-7 MARRIED COUPLES
Chaplain: Rev. W. McKenna
Organizers: Mr. & Mrs. A. Robinet
Leaders: Mr. & Mrs. R. McMahon

8-13 LEGION OF MARY
Chaplain: Rt. Rev. C. Carrigan, D.P.
Leader: Miss Mary Zdunich
Leader: Mrs. Wallace Nantais

14-17 SUMMER INSTITUTE FOR PRIESTS

18-20 MEN
Chaplain: Rev. M. F. White
Organizer: Mr. W. Green
B. Sacrament: Mr. P. Mailloux, leader
B. Sacrament: Mr. K. Philbin
Holy Name: Mr. Wm. Simpson
St. Paul: Mr. E. Meloche
St. Patrick: Mr. L. Pare
                Mr. T. Bannon
St. Joseph: Mr. C. Langlois
Precious Blood: Mr. F. Rocheleau
O.L. of Guadalupe: Mr. W. Lisinski
O. L. of the Rosary: Mr. S. Alexander
St. Michael: Mr. F. Weidel

22-24 LADIES OF ALL PARISHES (Mid-week)
Leader: Mrs. R. Walker

25-27 WOMEN
Chaplain: Rev. L. L. Ouellette
Organizer: Mrs. P. Goyeau
St. Clare: Miss A. Nosotti
St. Martin de Porres: Mrs. H. Harvieux
Christ the King: Miss Nora Ouellette
St. Gabriel: Mrs. E. Gomes
O.L. of Mt. Carmel: Mrs. J. Reddam

SEPTEMBER

2-4 MEN—Labour Day Retreat
Chaplain: Rev. J. M. Michon
Leader: Mr. C. Quenneville

8-10 WOMEN
Chaplain: Rev. V. C. Cote ▬▬▬
Organizer: Miss B. Jobagy ▬▬▬
Sacred Heart: Mrs. J. Dombroski ▬▬▬
St. Alphonsus: Miss V. Potvin ▬▬▬
I.C.C. Mrs. R. Lucier ▬▬▬
St. Anne: Mrs. M. Robertson ▬▬▬
St. Angela: Mrs. Norma Bagnarol ▬▬▬
St. Vladimir & Olga: Mrs. N. Kristalovich ▬▬
St. Michael: Miss C. Wolf ▬▬▬

15-17 MEN
Chaplain: Rev. R. G. Forton ▬▬▬
Amherstburg: Mr. P. Maitre, leader ▬▬▬
Amherstburg: Mr. L. Fox ▬▬▬
LaSalle: Mr. J. Beattie ▬▬▬
McGregor: Mr. H. Lucier ▬▬▬
River Canard: Mr. G. Beneteau ▬▬▬
Tecumseh: Mr. J. McKay ▬▬▬
Emeryville: Mr. L. Howell ▬▬▬
Belle River:
St. Vincent de Paul: Mr. J. McGibbon ▬▬▬

22-24 MEN
Chaplain: Rt. Rev. A. J. McNabb, D.P. ▬▬▬
Organizer: Mr. T. Daigneau ▬▬▬
Tilbury: Mr. G. Smith, leader ▬▬▬
Tilbury: Mr. E. Schramek ▬▬▬
Woodslee: Mr. R. Bissonnette ▬▬▬ Pl. Pk.
Comber:
Stevenson: Mr. L. Duquette ▬▬▬

29-1 MARRIED COUPLES
Chaplain: Rev. R. A. Charbonneau ▬▬▬
Organizer: Mr. & Mrs. A. Robinet ▬▬▬
Leaders: Mr. & Mrs. M. Perrault ▬▬▬

OCTOBER

6-9 STUDY DAYS FOR RELIGIOUS SUPERIORS

10-12 BRENNAN HIGH SCHOOL

13-15 BUSINESS WOMEN
Chaplain: Rev. J. G. Snyder ▬▬▬
Leaders: Miss Irene Duquette ▬▬▬
Miss Alice Serneels ▬▬▬

17-19 STUDENT NURSES OF CHATHAM

20-22 MARRIED COUPLES
Chaplain: Rev. R. E. Cartier ▬▬▬
Organizers: Mr & Mrs. A. Robinet ▬▬▬
Leaders: Mr. & Mrs. J. McMurdie ▬▬▬

23-24 DAIRYMEN
Leader: Mr. L. St. Antoine ▬▬▬

25 DAY OF RENEWAL FOR PRIESTS

27-29 MEN
Chaplain: Rev. F. Bezaire ▬▬▬
Organizer: Mr. T. Daigneau ▬▬▬
Chatham:
B. Sacrament: Mr. N. Belanger, leader ▬▬▬
Chatham: B. Sacrament: Mr. B. Hazzard ▬▬
Chatham: St. Joseph: Mr. J. Gerber ▬▬▬
Chatham: St. Ursula: Mr. D. Laurie ▬▬▬
Chatham: St. Agnes: Mr. G. Marlatt ▬▬▬
Blenheim: Mr. J. Kormendy ▬▬▬

Thamesville: Mr. J. Huys ▬▬▬
Prairie Siding: Mr. F. Bruette ▬▬▬
Tupperville: Mr. G. Tacq ▬▬▬
Merlin: Mr. H. Dillon ▬▬▬
Ridgetown: Mr. L. Deshaw ▬▬▬

NOVEMBER

3-5 RENEWAL DAYS FOR TEACHERS
Chaplain: Rev. J. Winter ▬▬▬
Leader: Mother Mary Charles

10-12 MEN
Chaplain: Rt. Rev. L. J. Phelan, D.P. ▬▬▬
Organizer: Mr. J. Namespetra ▬▬▬
Leamington: Mr. R. Gutteridge, leader ▬▬▬
Leamington: Mr. M. Eagen ▬▬▬
Harrow: Mr. G. Pouget ▬▬▬
Kingsville: Mr. J. Bachmeier ▬▬▬
Essex: Mr. E. Matis ▬▬▬
Maidstone: Mr. J. Hebert ▬▬▬
Wheatley: Mr. G. Heyens ▬▬▬

14-16 STUDENTS

17-19 LES HOMMES DE WINDSOR ET DE L'OUEST DU COMTE D'ESSEX
Aumonier: Rt. Rev. A. Caron, D.P. ▬▬▬
Organizateur: M. E. Bondy ▬▬▬
Tecumseh: M. Louis Lachance, Chef ▬▬▬
Tecumseh: M. Wm. St. Pierre ▬▬▬
LaSalle: M. Ubald Ducharme ▬▬▬
River Canard: M. Harry Delisle ▬▬▬
St. Gregory: M. Arthur Wilder ▬▬▬ Pl. Pk. 931

20-22 UNIVERSITY OF DETROIT BOYS

24-26 MEN
Chaplain: Rev. J. P. Boyde ▬▬▬
Organizer: Mr. T. Daigneau ▬▬▬
Wallaceburg:
H. Family: Mr. T. Lozon, leader ▬▬▬
H. Family: Mr. E. Yazbeck ▬▬▬
O.L. Help of C. Mr. M. Van Damme ▬▬▬
Mr. N. Baertsoen ▬▬▬
Port Lambton: Mr. L. Murphy ▬▬▬

DECEMBER

1-3 LES HOMMES DU COMTE DE KENT ET DE L'EST DU COMTE D'ESSEX
Aumonier: M. l'Abbe R. Beneteau ▬▬▬
Organizateur: M. E. Bondy ▬▬▬
Paincourt: M. J. Richer, chef ▬▬▬
Paincourt: M. N. Roy ▬▬▬
Tilbury: M. A. Pinsonneault ▬▬▬
Stoney Point: M. Hiram Roy ▬▬▬
Staples: M. G. Barrette ▬▬▬ Woods. 15-21
Stevenson: M. Louis Benoit ▬▬▬
St. Joachim: M. T. Sylvestre ▬▬▬
Comber: M. Leo Lacharite ▬▬▬ 144-R-21
Emeryville: M. E. Campeau ▬▬▬
Belle River: M. D. Gagnier ▬▬▬ 73-R-11

8-10 LES JEUNES FILLES QUI TRAVAILLENT
Aumonier: M. l'Abbe C. Lanove ▬▬▬
Organizateur: Mlle. Cecile Beneteau ▬▬▬
Chef: Mlle M. Nadeau ▬▬▬

Appendix 5: Dedication Plaques on the Retreat House Grounds

	Item	*Dedication*
1.	Yoke	"Come to me all you who are burdened. I will refresh you" Rev. M. A. Johnston

2.	Sign outside Nazareth	In celebration of Anna Chaychuk 95th Birthday Mother of Vicki ULLYETT

3.	Stool outside door of St. Mary's	Those we love don't go away, they walk beside us every day. Unseen, unheard, but always near, so loved, so missed, so very dear.

4.	Plaque next to stool	In Memory of Our Dear Friend Betty Ann Who was an inspiration to many.

5.	Bench outside St. Mary's	Sister Rose Marie Rau In Recognition of her many years of Devoted Service The Midwest Conference August 2006

6.	Holy Family Statue	Holy Family Group GIFT Dr. & Mrs. Beuglet's Family

7.	Plaque Tree outside chapel	This tree honours a Loving Mother & Faithful Friend RITA MAYRAND Who went home to her God May 12, 1993 THE STAFF

Item	*Dedication*
8. Plaque outside Christ the King Chapel	COMMEMORATING OUR 35ᵀᴴ ANNIVERSARY MAR. 16, 1996 JOHN BRAZILL CIRCLE # 1385 COLUMBIAN SQUIRES MCGREGOR, ONT.
9. Plaque outside Christ the King Chapel	IN MEMORY OF FATHER PAT MACCANN ONTARIO PROVINCIAL COLUMBIAN SQUIRES SENATORS CLUB AUG. 1995
10. On "Conference Room" sign outside St. Joseph's	IN CELEBRATION OF 40 YEARS OF PRIESTHOOD FR. DES SCANLAN, C.Ss.R. MARGARET & AUSTIN GRAVELLE 2000
11. Tree in yard near house	THIS TREE IS PLANTED IN MEMORY OF MARVENNA BRENNAN TRAHER IN A PLACE THAT SHE LOVED, HOLY FAMILY RETREAT HOUSE SEPTEMBER 1920 – APRIL 2001
12. Plaque at S.W.corner of house 	THIS GARDEN FLOURISHES ON THESE HOLY GROUNDS. IN GRATITUDE FOR PERSONAL GROWTH ... A GIFT OF LIFE BILL C., WILLIAM K., PEARCE M.
13. Plaque in front of small tree S. of house	IN GRATITUDE FOR THE LIVES OF TWO BOARD MEMBERS FR. RAY RENAUD LEO GAUTHIER WHO WENT HOME TO GOD IN 2004

Item	Dedication

14. Stone between 3 trees S. of house

IN MEMORY OF
SERGE "DODONG" DIOSO
10/22/85 (red heart) 4/25/03
U OF D JESUITS
CLASS 2003
HE'S RAPPIN' WITH
THE ANGELS NOW

15. 2 Stone benches
16. near fence E. of house

IN MEMORY OF
SERGE B. DIOSO
OCTOBER 22, 1985 – APRIL 25, 2003
U OF D JESUITS – CLASS 2003

17. Small BVM shrine on fence E. of house

LORD,
WITH YOU, VICKIE
HAS MADE THESE
HOLY GROUNDS BEAUTIFUL
KEEP HER IN YOUR HEART!
AMEN

18. Tree in middle of yard

THIS TREE IS PLANTED
TO HONOUR 15 YEARS
OF LIFE AND MIRACLES
MIDWEST CONFERENCE
1992

19. Tree in yard

DEDICATED TO
LARRY ALLEN
A LIVING EXAMPLE OF
"THE GIVING TREE"
JAN. 3, 1998
HOUSE OF SHALOM YOUTH
  CENTRE

20. Tree in yard

MID WEST CONFERENCE
20TH ANNIVERSARY
AT
HOLY FAMILY RETREAT HOUSE
AUGUST 1997

Index

Bold entries indicate pictures.